SOME ASSEMBLY REQUIRED

A Guide to Savvy Parenting

Richard Lazaroff, MD

LifeRich Publishing is a registered trademark of The Reader's Digest Association, Inc.

LifeRich Publishing books may be ordered through booksellers or by contacting:

LifeRich Publishing
1663 Liberty Drive
Bloomington, IN 47403
www.liferichpublishing.com
1 (888) 238-8637

ISBN: 978-1-4897-1534-0 (sc)
ISBN: 978-1-4897-1535-7 (hc)
ISBN: 978-1-4897-1533-3 (e)

Library of Congress Control Number: 2018900572

Print information available on the last page.

LifeRich Publishing rev. date: 04/02/2018

To all the families over the years
that placed their trust in me to care for their children.

Dr. L

Contents

Introduction

Congratulations! If you are reading this book, the chances are you are expecting or already have a child. The parenting journey you have embarked on is one that will be a life-changing experience, but when going somewhere new, guidelines are often helpful. While this book is not intended to provide a roadmap or directions to success, per se, it will help you avoid the potholes along the way.

Parents need books that address everyday health concerns in children: a comprehensive reference for vaccinations, well-child care, and symptoms of infection and disease. Although *Some Assembly Required* will not be that book, at times it will discuss some of those topics to illustrate and explain those matters and others. *Some Assembly Required* will also provide links and references for resources in print and on the web that might prove useful for those wanting more information. Unfortunately, while the web is full of information, not all of the information is well vetted and some of it may make parents unnecessarily anxious, so caution is advised.

I recently retired from 35 years in pediatric practice and, with my wife, have raised two children of my own. This book is intended to share my personal and professional experiences and lessons learned with humor, guidance and, I hope, wisdom about what often lies just beneath the everyday challenges of parenthood. Many of the chapters begin with an actual office encounter or phone call. Those encounters and phone calls serve as a starting point to investigate matters more meaningfully as I recall some of the very things I said to patients on a daily basis that seemed most helpful.

Some Assembly Required is a reflection of my experience and my opinions, the latter of which, like all opinions, may be considered seriously or rejected entirely. Please share some of these discussions with those you trust—your parents, your friends, and even your pediatrician. We all come to the experience of raising children with different values, and it is not my wish or place (nor is it anyone else's) to impose my values on you. Over the course of my years of practice, parents would often ask me, "What would you do if it were your child?" I would respond to their inquiry, but with the caveat that my answer would reflect my values and that they might differ from their own. Please know that while I will address this question at times in my book, my responses, again, are not necessarily to be taken as the last, or only, word.

Since this book starts with infancy and goes through the adolescent years, you might wonder how to read it if now pregnant for the first time or already raising children of various ages. I would suggest that all parents consider reading it start to finish as the conversation builds on past stages culminating in the high stakes but enormous opportunities that face parents today when making choices to successfully and savvily raise an adolescent. Then I would put in on the shelf and re-visit it from time to time.

Now, let's get started!

Chapter 1

TAKING EMOTIONAL INVENTORY AND RECOGNIZING YOUR ASPIRATIONS FOR YOUR CHILD

Most children will be raised by two very different people who have chosen to become a family unit. They may have different ethnic backgrounds, education, experiences with children, and childhood memories.

Most couples I know did not focus on their differences when they chose to commit to each other. More often, they saw their shared interests and shared opinions as more significant in their relationship.

I do not think my wife and I, or many of my patients, for that matter, made an *intentional* effort to discuss how we were raised. How was discipline handled, did the family have a commitment to serve the community charitably, what was the role of exercise versus the role of sedentary activities like television watching, what was the role of grandparents and other extended-family members, how important was money, were family dinners a regular occurrence, and how were feelings discussed or handled—these and other topics were not part and parcel of our discussions.

Though some children will be raised in a single parent home, it is no less important for a single parent to understand their childhood and how their experiences and memories will translate into both strengths and weaknesses as a parent. Sometimes it is helpful for a single parent to "bounce off" some of their feelings with another adult in their life to heighten their own self-awareness.

Some religions require couples to complete courses on understanding their differences prior to marriage. Though some topics in these courses touch upon such considerations as having and raising children, such deliberations are really too far off for most couples to understand how crucial understanding their differences will be when making choices together.

A good place to start this conversation would be to read a book on the topic, *Parenting from the Inside Out,* by Daniel Siegel and Mary Hartzell. In the book, the authors stress how important it is for parents to assess their own experiences from childhood, both good and bad. It is not necessarily about whether you experienced a "happy" childhood or one with unusual stress. It is more about "knowing" yourself and the potential for having unresolved issues that could lead to history repeating itself. After all, who does not have unresolved issues? This internal understanding that Siegel and Hartzell describe allows parents to be more available to connect to their children in a healthy fashion, living in the present, respecting their children as individuals, remaining flexible and thoughtful when facing challenging choices, and continuing to grow as people. Studies show that parents who "know" themselves are more likely to raise children who feel a positive attachment to their parents.

Ultimately, as parents, we are striving for a healthy balance between being attached to our children and giving them the opportunity to explore the world independently. Sometimes economic factors play a role in adult children coming back to live in the household, but if your adult children end up living in your basement for "too many years" (I call that failure to launch), you probably missed the mark a little despite what were no doubt your best efforts. Healthy attachment can only take place when a parent or parents are emotionally available and aware of their own strengths and weaknesses. Achieving this emotional stability has less to do with the individual traumas and successes of one's own childhood than with understanding them. When I saw families struggling to let go in a healthy fashion, I often saw a parent or parents with unmanaged fears and anxieties making decisions to enable rather than "help" their children grow into capable adults, or choosing to become emotionally enmeshed with their child when their own marriage or other relationships did not meet their emotional needs. When I saw families letting go in a healthy fashion, I saw a parent or parents who were working to overcome their anxieties (we all have them) and were intentionally supplying needed support while allowing their children room to make a few mistakes and develop adult coping skills.

I think most people assume, between the love they feel for their child and their natural capabilities as people, that raising children successfully will be straightforward. It is anything but. Though we all fear influences and experiences beyond our control causing problems for our kids (for example, events befalling our children outside the home), my experience over the last three decades tells me something else. Who we are in our own homes and how we react as parents is where the money is, so to speak. It is imperative to get to know yourself and your partner (if applicable) and to understand each other's values and upbringing before trying to successfully raise children of your own. And remember, if you are reading this now and already have children beyond the years of infancy, it is never too late to do this "work", to get to "know" yourself, and to "grow" as people so that you can become a better person and a better parent.

Chapter 2

LIFE WITH AN INFANT

It is three AM and I hear my three-month old daughter crying in her crib. I am working the next day and often do not go into help since she is breast fed anyway. This night I get up and go in to change her diaper and bring her to my wife. She is wiggling around on the changing table and smiling at me. I feel very happy.

What will life be like?

My wife received a call from my daughter one day. She is now a first-time mother of a four-month-old boy and is doing a beautiful job. She is also a lawyer and will be going back to work soon. Toward the end of the phone call, she said, "I cannot wait to get my life back!" My wife informed her that that will never happen. We all had a good laugh.

Having a child changes everything. I mean, EVERYTHING. I think the first big realization of this for me was how most of what drove me crazy in my relationship with my parents stemmed from the excessive love that they, like most parents, felt for their child. This love can take bizarre forms that interfere with the nurturing relationship most of us desire. But properly dispensed, parental love provides the foundation for the trust, intimacy, self-esteem, competence and empathy that most of us desire for our children to develop.

When my daughter said she wanted her life back, I think she was referring to the rhythm and predictability of work, time with her spouse and time for herself. One must acknowledge very quickly that these life activities

4

are all pretty time consuming, and a resetting of priorities must take place. Parents who aspire to be perfect at all of them can become anxious or they can choose to accept their best efforts at each of these demands as good enough. Perhaps individually, or as couple, you just feel overwhelmed. If that is the case, discuss this feeling with your pediatrician and they can often direct you to community resources or give you suggestions to manage your days more successfully.

Post-partum depression is different than just feeling overwhelmed or anxious. It is a very real medical problem peaking at about four months after birth. Your doctor will usually have you complete a screening questionnaire in the office to see if you are having any difficulties and will refer you for treatment if you are clinically depressed.

A few practical matters to consider when you first come home from the hospital:

1. Do not write all your thank-you notes right away.
2. Silence your cellphone when the baby is napping as you will also need some sleep.
3. Tell your best friend to put out the word that you are not ready for visitors. If you ever ran over to a friend's home in the first days after a new baby, well, you were mostly a nuisance. New moms and new dads are exhausted and need not entertain even those who truly want to see the baby or show how much they care about you. If they would like to bring dinner, they can drop it off and go.
4. Let others help both of you. There are many ways for a grandparent or a friend to be helpful. If breastfeeding, you will be the only one feeding the infant, but others can change diapers, do the laundry, grocery shop, give a bath, or help put the baby down to sleep.

Is my baby O.K.?

Almost all parents experience some level of fear and anxiety when they step back into the house for the first time with a new baby from the hospital. They set the baby on the floor in their car seat and wonder, "Now what do we do?" Does the baby's cry mean they are hungry? Sleepy? In need of a diaper change? Could the baby just be worried that mom and dad have not contributed the maximum to their 401K plan? (Just kidding.) Newborns, on average, cry 2-3 hours per day. They are in a new and very stimulating environment that is different than the womb. Remember, it's a learning curve for them, too. Be patient as time is your ally.

Parents have fears about everything being all right with their newborn and whether they are going to be able to tell if their child needs medical attention. After all, most of us have studied and been trained to do our daily jobs. Suddenly, the most important job of one's life is upon us and we wonder if we will be good at it.

I remember the day that my son commented that even normal breathing in his first child worried him. Newborns do breathe in a periodic fashion where pauses of up to 10 seconds can be followed by rapid, short breaths. Most first-time parents find this frightening. These "fears" are not pathological, such as those we will consider in our next section, and can still be brought to your pediatrician's attention. Such calls should be welcomed and understood by your doctor. If not, think twice about whether you have selected the right place to receive your pediatric care. Reassurance about similar concerns will allow you to develop the confidence you will need and become more and more certain of your own abilities.

Sometimes parents have a medical reason to be extra anxious about an infant. Perhaps there is a family history of SIDS (Sudden Infant Death Syndrome), or the baby had to spend a brief period in an ICU (intensive-care unit) for, say, respiratory problems. Fairly common occurrences such as a low Apgar score at birth do not overly concern most medical providers who, based on their knowledge, experience, and training, know this is not a significant concern moving forward. But parents, without this medical background, worry. And these feeling do not have to originate from concerns about your own baby. They may come from a worrisome medical story about a neighbor, friend, or an acquaintance's child. When such worries take up too much energy, parents can feel deprived of the very enjoyment of their baby they were looking forward to. In extreme cases, this excessive worry can lead to what is known as vulnerable child syndrome (Morris Green, 1964).

There are so many stories I could tell here about the many vulnerable children I saw during my career. Because it is one of the most important concepts I will discuss in this book, I think a couple would be helpful.

A first-time mother was well known to me as I was her pediatrician from the time of her own birth. As an adolescent, she was diagnosed and treated for an anxiety disorder. She seemed thrilled when her child was born, but over the first few months I received almost daily phone calls and frequent visits due to concerns about the baby's breathing, color, spitting up, bowel movements, and a vague uneasiness about whether the baby was developing normally neurologically. For a short period of time, the parents decided it was best for a cousin to take over all care of the infant.

There had been no special events in the woman's pregnancy and no problems with the child's birth. In fact, despite 15-20 office visits during the child's first six months of life, a true medical diagnosis was never made for any of the perceived problems. Fortunately, just making the diagnosis of vulnerable child syndrome, having a mother who was open to receiving medical treatment for an anxiety disorder, and allowing for some time to pass, enabled this mother to enjoy her child in a healthier manner.

In another case, a young couple with a six-month old chose me as their pediatrician. Not unlike our previous parent, this family had many "medical" concerns about their infant and followed through on them with countless office visits and phone calls. Despite numerous examinations and reassurances, the family continued this pattern of frequent visits without a significant diagnosis being made. I suspected this was a vulnerable child but could not pinpoint the reason. At one visit, I was alone briefly with the mother and asked if there was something in the couple's history that I was "missing." She told me that she and her husband had been pregnant once prior to their marriage and had chosen to place the child for adoption. Upon being made aware of this, I realized it was entirely reasonable for the parents to be more anxious and I also recognized that they may need time or some help to deal successfully with their feelings about the adoption.

This last patient I will describe was actually the first child I ever saw with this problem. He was nearly 10 years old, and I was his fourth or fifth pediatrician. No one had successfully allayed his parents' fears about multiple medical issues despite many tests, trips to specialists, and multiple diagnoses made over the years, all accompanied with different treatments. When I became involved, the primary complaint was a persistent cough. In the course of taking his medical history, I learned that in his first days of life he had required oxygen briefly for a breathing problem. His mother indicated to me that she thought he was going to die. After a complete examination, which turned up nothing abnormal, and a review of recent testing performed by the boy's last pediatrician, I informed the mother that we should consider a diagnosis of vulnerable child syndrome. Skepticism on her part ultimately became acceptance and a relief to all. No additional testing or medications were required.

Your pediatrician might suspect this diagnosis, but parents sometimes hide how difficult it can be to see their own child in a "normal" fashion. Thus, it can be a hard diagnosis for a pediatrician to make because it may seem judgmental. I have found that just acknowledging these feelings often allows a parent to move forward in a healthier fashion. In fact, it became my routine to discuss this diagnosis "preventively" with parents when, from my experience, I thought they might be at risk. An example would be in a baby finally going home after having to stay extra days in the NICU (neonatal intensive care unit). Parents really appreciated knowing that these feelings were common ("normal") and most accepted the challenge to overcome them. Rarely, counseling may be needed to work through these emotions.

At times in my career, I sensed anxiety on the part of new parents related to being judged by grandparents on either or both sides. Surprising at first to me, there were some children who had never been to my office without the grandparents tagging along. One of my favorite lines to new parents was, "It's now your chance to screw up your own children." Just kidding of course, but you may need to ask grandma and grandpa to back off. This is your turn. As I mentioned in Chapter One, you will need to take inventory on how each of you was raised and make your own *intentional* decisions about how you will raise your child.

Is my baby OK? Managing anxiety is a common challenge for parents of a new baby. It is a major driver of physician visits and can lead to unnecessary medical testing and interventions. Parents need to recognize the sources of their anxiety as there is usually not something wrong with the baby. Most times, pediatricians need to simply listen and offer support rather than labeling these concerns with a diagnosis like reflux, food allergy, or milk intolerance. Your pediatrician will be alert to the signs and symptoms of true medical disorders and will be quick to order appropriate testing or refer your family to a pediatric subspecialist. But more times than not, your baby is OK and that reassurance from your doctor should be sufficient.

There are also community resources like Parents as Teachers that can be invaluable in supporting new parents (https://parentsasteachers.org). This parent education service is free and provides personal and group meetings aimed at optimizing early development and providing reassurance that you are on the right track with your baby.

What do you need at home in the way of "stuff"?

As an expectant family, you will become aware seemingly overnight of an entire industry marketing its products to you. Just as with cars and houses, there are bells and whistles you may want but that may not be necessary.

Take breastfeeding. In all likelihood, you will be self-motivated or convinced by your pediatrician to breastfeed. This decision has health benefits for your baby (improved immunity), allows for feelings of attachment to develop, saves money, is convenient, and is, after all, nature's way. And science is likely to continue to find additional benefits from breastfeeding.

However, even breastfed babies should take a bottle from time to time to free up mom and allow the baby's father the enjoyment of feeding the baby. Waiting too long to introduce a bottle to an "exclusively" breastfed baby can result in a baby who will not take a bottle at all. (I was never able to give my first child a bottle as we waited a bit too long before introduction.) I advise parents of breastfed babies to try a bottle at about two weeks of age and to continue to offer a bottle a couple of times a week throughout the duration of nursing. It is easy for a baby to "get out of the habit" of taking a bottle and this can be very frustrating. You will need to buy bottles and nipples, but there is no one brand necessarily better than any other though some companies market their nipple as more like mother's (NUK) or have designs said to reduce air/gas intake (Dr. Brown's).

For all the benefits of breastfeeding, please remember, though breastfeeding is a great choice, choosing to exclusively bottle feed with formula is perfectly acceptable and the best choice for some families. Parents often asked me if I was pro-breast or pro-bottle feeding. My answer was that I was pro-parent. Do not allow pressure to breast feed from family, friends, or your pediatrician to dictate your decision.

A thermometer is a must. For a newborn, it should be a digital thermometer that can be used rectally or in the armpit. A fever is a temperature of 100.4 degrees Fahrenheit or higher and for children under 2-3 months of age is a reason to speak to your pediatrician immediately. At this age, infants with fever will need to be examined. It is not sound medical advice to administer acetaminophen and observe an infant under three months of age at home until the next day.

A crib meeting current safety standards or a bassinet should be used for sleeping. (Boxinettes are making a comeback, with some hospitals discharging infants with this inexpensive but safer alternative to sleeping with a parent.) The mattress should be firm, and the infant needs to be placed on their back and without bumper pads or additional items in the crib. The American Academy of Pediatrics believes that infants sleeping in the same room as their parents for the first 6-12 months have some reduction in SIDS, though it is not clear what the mechanism of the reduction is. The AAP, however, is not suggesting you need to watch your child sleep so that you can intervene if the baby stops breathing (though I believe that is how many parents will take this advice). After all, you too will need to sleep, and you must remember that SIDS is a very rare event. *I have a lot of concern that this recommendation will only increase anxiety about the 24/7 nature of your responsibility to your child.* Stay tuned as others do share my opinion and I suspect that this recommendation may change. (http://pediatrics.aappublications.org/content/early/2016/10/20/peds.2016-2938)

Co-sleeping is a no-no. This unquestionably increases the risk of SIDS and, additionally, creates a situation where the child learns to fall asleep only with the parent present. This can be a hard habit to break and will often lead to what Dr. Richard Ferber, in his book *Solve Your Child's Sleep Problems,* calls trained night-criers as the parent becomes an attachment item.

Medications in the home at this time can be limited to acetaminophen for fever in infants under six months and either acetaminophen or ibuprofen for those over six months. Vitamin D supplementation is recommended for all newborns to prevent rickets (poor bone mineralization), for which newborns are at special risk because of their limited sun exposure and insufficient supplies of Vitamin D in breast milk. Formulas are Vitamin D fortified, but even bottle-fed babies should receive Vitamin D until they are consuming 32 ounces of formula a day (usually around the age of 2-3 months). Cough and cold mediations are of no value to children under five years of age and may even cause side effects. Gas drops, the subject of numerous studies, have been shown to provide no consistent medical benefit. A bulb syringe and the appropriate amount of nasal saline solution may help clear an infant's nose when colds cause congestion.

Obviously, one needs diapers and barrier creams (containing zinc oxide) for common diaper rashes. Some diapers are super absorbent and can be useful at night and when battling diaper rash.

A cool-mist vaporizer is a good investment. When your baby's first cold comes, it will help keep the nasal secretions thin and help the baby breathe more easily.

Last, a car seat is a must and the law. Whether it is integrated with your stroller, snaps into the car, or can be used in multiple vehicles, it comes in options for all budgets and preferences.

This list is not meant to be exhaustive. While you may *want* to have such items as baby swings, bathing accessories, and strollers, these are not items you will *need* to have. Remember that when infants spend too much time in confining equipment such as car seats, strollers, swings, and exersaucers, their motor development can be slowed.

It's easy to be taken with new technologies, which promise to make looking after your baby ever easier and more reassuring. But do these devices deliver the goods? Video monitors are expensive, and unless your home is quite large, you will probably hear your baby easily when they wake from sleep, so they may be an unnecessary expense. And while watching can be fun, depending on the parent, it can produce anxiety. I would suggest seeing if you can get by without one. Devices that monitor a baby's vital signs (socks with the ability to measure oxygenation, for example) take this potential anxiety issue to another level. As for heart-rate and breathing monitors, only rarely will an infant need to be sent home with such devices, and this type of medical decision should be made by your physician or neonatologist (a hospital doctor specializing in the care of sick newborns). The use of monitors outside of such recommendations will likely result in false alarms and unnecessary emergency visits and medical testing. Though marketed as devices that empower parents, these technologies' potential for harm may, I believe, outweigh their presumed benefits for some families.

Vaccinations

The science behind immunization is quite sound, with adverse vaccination events very rare. The individual child and society at large benefit dramatically from the protection immunizations provide. Those who choose not to vaccinate are counting on the rest of the community's being vaccinated to create herd immunity, thus allowing for these diseases to remain rare. However, recent studies have demonstrated that herd immunity can break down rapidly when parents choose not to vaccinate their children. In addition, none of our vaccines are capable of conferring 100% protection. For example, the pertussis vaccine (whooping cough) is only 80-85% protective. Both of these factors, parents choosing not to immunize and not having perfect vaccines, contribute to "outbreaks" of serious, preventable diseases.

While pregnant, you should have received a Tdap vaccine (tetanus, diphtheria, pertussis) and an influenza vaccine if it was flu season. The Tdap given during pregnancy is primarily to help protect your baby from pertussis until the baby can be fully immunized. Additionally, mothers are the most common reservoir for spreading this infection to an infant. Pertussis is devastating in a young baby, as coughing fits lead to poor oxygenation and potential brain injury. The influenza vaccine is given because influenza can be very hard on pregnant women. Grandparents and other caregivers should get the Tdap vaccine as well, before the infant is born.

Some parents are under the impression that once babies have their first shots they are safe to go out more in public. This is not true. Babies have insufficient immunity, and, therefore, incomplete protection against any of the diseases represented in these vaccines after a single dose. It is only after completing the whole series of vaccinations that immunity is good, though it is never 100%. Furthermore, most illnesses babies "catch" by going out in public are caused by other viruses and infectious diseases for which we do not currently immunize.

I recommend against unnecessary exposure in public for the baby until 2-3 months of age. Since a child's immune system is somewhat immature prior to this age, infections can quickly become more serious. Additionally, it can be more difficult at these young ages for your pediatrician to be reassured about sick, febrile infants simply by taking a good history and examining them. Predicting which infants with fever have serious bacterial infections is harder in these young infants, with the result that it is often necessary to perform additional testing, and at times, even hospitalization.

Some vaccines, especially PCV 13 (for pneumococcal infections), have dramatically reduced the frequency of ear and other respiratory infections, thereby reducing the use of antibiotics. This single vaccine may have been the biggest advance seen in the course of my pediatric career, as no longer do pediatricians see child after child with ear infections. The reduction in antibiotic use is a bonus, as overuse of these drugs has been shown to contribute to "superbugs" (resistant bacterial infections).

Random internet websites are not where you should go for immunization information. Two trusted sites are immunize.org and chop.edu. Since your pediatrician is required to obtain informed consent before vaccinating your child, ask as many questions at your visit as you want.

My experience is that there is a subset of parents that do not want much modern medical care. Many in this group seem to "fear" that by consenting to a vaccine that only in the rarest of circumstances can have side effects, they may actively participate in potentially injuring their own child. These parents seem to put little mental energy into considering the injury that can occur if their child gets these preventable diseases or passes them along to others. Additionally, this hesitancy about vaccines may be a reflection of a general mistrust that often interferes with the development of a healthy doctor-patient relationship.

In describing this fear of vaccination, some parents still cite concerns about the supposed link between vaccines and autism. This concern has received close scientific scrutiny and there has been NO LINK established between receiving vaccines and developing autism (See ncbi.nlm.nih.gov/pubmed/24814559). In fact, the latest research suggests that genetics plays the primary role in the development of this disorder. Despite this evidence, many parents still choose to believe incorrect information when these myths are presented alongside the facts perhaps because they are more familiar with the misinformation as it is so prevalent in our social media.

Parents who refuse vaccines can really be a challenge to a doctor. Nationally, for some time now, pediatricians have been pushing the AAP to adopt policies that would allow for the dismissal from the pediatrician's practice of families that refuse immunizations. Recently, the AAP has stated that taking such action is acceptable as a last resort. As a working pediatrician, I always felt that these children needed a medical home, like all children, and perhaps even more so. I simply made it clear to families that I would continue to respectfully discuss vaccines at every opportunity and found that most parents came around over time. However, if not vaccinating their child was part of a general mistrust that could not be overcome, I found it was occasionally necessary to part ways in the hope that another pediatrician might be a better fit.

Sleep and schedules

At one visit several years ago, a mother informed me that her four-month-old infant did not like her crib and was sleeping very poorly, prompting me to ask if her child had spoken of this dislike, or had she tweeted or texted this information to her.

Many new parents struggle with getting their baby on a reasonable sleep schedule. Perhaps it would be helpful to understand some of the basics of sleep before engaging in some ideas about what parents can do to develop a schedule and a good sleep routine. A great reference is Dr. Richard Ferber's book, *Solve Your Child's Sleep Problems*.

Most infants have sleep cycles of about 45 minutes. Normal sleep cycles have periods of light and deep sleep. This means that every 45 minutes the child will be in light sleep and might wake if hungry, uncomfortable, or if trained always to fall asleep with assistance (feeding, rocking, pacifier, music). Training the child to fall asleep on their own is desirable for most families. Certainly, one can look for opportunities to put even newborns down to bed, sleepy but awake (and alone). However, aggressive sleep training, where your baby will likely cry until asleep, should probably wait until several months of age. I consider sleeping through the night as eight consecutive hours of sleep (10 P.M.-6 A.M.), something most infants can achieve by four months of age and certainly by six months.

When this has not occurred by six months, usually it is a matter of having to break a habit of feeding your infant until they are asleep or using transitional objects (pacifier) or attachment behaviors (such as rocking). Some better attachment items (a small, soft lovey, for example) are those the child can find on their own easily. However, even these small objects can contribute to an increased risk of sudden infant death syndrome (SIDS) and are best avoided.

My advice about sleep and schedules when taking a newborn home is:

1. If your baby is fussy and has not fed in the last two hours, feed them.
2. If your baby has slept more than three hours between 6 A.M. and 11 P.M., wake them. This will help in getting their days and nights switched to match your own. Remember, during pregnancy your movement during the day made the child sleep, and when you became still at night, they would awaken.
3. Do not be afraid to put a baby down if fussy and recently fed. They may be tired. You can rock them and use a pacifier when they are very young, but even this is not necessary. As they get older (over two months), give them 5-10 minutes to fall asleep without any assistance. Ultimately, this will allow them to learn to put themselves back to sleep in the middle of the night when they find themselves sleepy but awake and alone.
4. When a baby cries out after a single sleep cycle (approximately 40-45 minutes), they may be able to put themselves back to sleep without being fed and without parental involvement. Always consider this possibility and give them a few minutes to self-settle again.

Most babies have a schedule that emerges over the first four months, so do not be afraid to start watching the clock for patterns. If most mornings they wake at 6 and go down for a nap around 8:30, put them down the next day at 8:30 and get some things done in your own life.

How do I know if my baby is sick?

Once I came home from work and my wife told me she thought the dog was sick. I asked why she thought this was so, and she told me he was not wagging his tail. I often use that story with parents when examining a child who looks quite good despite reasonable concerns of the parent that they may be "sick"—there the child is on my exam table, playful, smiling, cooing, and wagging their tail.

Babies are very predictable in their feedings. If they feed poorly twice in a row, it should be considered that they may be sick. Other signs suggesting illness are diminished activity or having a bothersome symptom such as a rash, vomiting, diarrhea, cough, extreme fussiness, or shortness of breath. If any of these occur, you should speak to your doctor.

If your baby is warm to the touch, take their temperature. A temperature of 100.4 Fahrenheit or higher is a fever regardless of where it is taken. If the child is under three months of age, they need to be examined immediately. If they are older than three months, it may be appropriate to give them acetaminophen and observe them for additional symptoms. Fevers during the first year of life that last 72 hours should always be reported to your physician's office and may necessitate an office visit. Fevers of shorter duration at this age that are accompanied by one of the bothersome symptoms listed above should also be reported. Teething is never a reasonable explanation for a temperature greater than 100.4. Please do not accept that answer from anyone, including medical personnel.

Jaundice

I once received a call from a new father that his newborn (home barely 24 hours) was jaundiced (whites of the eyes appearing yellow). The father grew up down the street from me and called for reassurance even though I was no longer in practice. It reminded me that newborn jaundice, an event that occurs in almost 60% of babies, is often the first time that new parents call their doctor about what they perceive to be a medical problem.

Most of the time jaundice is not harmful, especially in healthy, full-term infants. Jaundice is caused by the excessive production or reduced elimination of the compound bilirubin by the body. All of us, including newborns, are removing red blood cells (RBC) from the body every day and replacing them with new RBCs made in the bone marrow. Bilirubin is a byproduct of the body's destroying these older red blood cells. Normally bilirubin is removed (conjugated) by the liver; however, the liver does not work as well in the first week of life, thus making jaundice common. In addition, jaundice can be accentuated by differences between the infant's and mother's blood types, problems getting breastfeeding established, prematurity, and a host of other reasons.

In all my years of practice, I never once cared for a child harmed by an elevated level of bilirubin in the newborn period. But I still found it necessary to explain this type of potential injury to the brain (kernicterus) in order to get parents to understand why blood tests, and at times, treatment was needed.

O.K., so we get this phone call or see a jaundiced infant in the office. What do we tell the parent? Do we discuss possible brain damage even though it is exceedingly rare (yes, one needs to be a straight shooter)? Do we draw blood to measure the bilirubin (yes, sometimes)? Do we treat the elevated bilirubin with phototherapy (again, sometimes necessary, if the level is too high for a given age in days)? Can breastfeeding be allowed to safely continue (almost always yes, however very rarely, breast feeding may need to be interrupted for 24 hours in a case of breast milk jaundice), or do we need to supplement breast milk with formula (maybe, if the infant has lost 10% of their body weight since birth)?

The reason I chose to discuss this topic is not so much to define the levels of bilirubin that might require treatment or to frighten parents about kernicterus, an extremely rare type of brain damage that can occur in a newborn with severe jaundice. It is more to acknowledge that this may be the first opportunity for parents and their physician to work together on a "medical problem". Almost always, jaundice will get better on its own by one week of age when the liver is working well and breastfeeding is going great. But until then, this interaction about newborn jaundice may serve as a template for a good therapeutic relationship moving forward. Some of the information you will receive from your pediatrician may sound serious, even alarming, as a good pediatrician keeps no secrets from parents. But often the medical care plan will simply consist of "watchful waiting" versus active treatment (this will be true for many future concerns as well). Both parties, doctor and parent, may need to stay in touch, communicate by phone, or follow up in the office. Parents must listen carefully (jaundice is usually not serious!) or they may have their emotions and anxieties hijack their ability to follow simple medical advice about feedings, follow-up visits, or when additional blood tests are needed.

These days most doctors will send you home with a summary of your office visit so that you can review the diagnosis and treatment plan when you get home. But while in the office, ask questions until you are comfortable with all the information you receive.

Colic

A small percentage of infants will be diagnosed with colic. In the words of my three-year-old (pediatrician-in-waiting?) grandson, the cause of colic is a "mystery", a term he likes to use when a cause and effect are not obvious. Infants fuss and cry to communicate sensations of hunger, tiredness, gas, and difficulties dealing with what can be a very stimulating environment (especially in comparison to the womb). But when crying spells are prolonged (longer than three hours), predictable (late afternoon and early evening), and persistent (last more than three weeks), often a diagnosis of colic is made. Colic does not start until about two weeks of age and usually resolves itself without treatment over several weeks to several months (almost all babies "outgrow" colic by four months).

If you think your child is colicky, your first move should be to see your pediatrician for an examination to make sure there is no physical problem causing the excessive crying. Once reassured, you can expect your doctor to advise a stepwise progression of techniques to soothe your baby. Dr. Harvey Karp's book, *The Happiest Baby on the Block,* provides good advice, with its 5 S's—Swaddle, Side or Stomach, Shush, Swing, and Suck. If your baby has not slept in the last 2-3 hours and it is not time to eat, consider putting the baby down in the crib to sleep, as frequently a colicky infant is just overly tired.

There is some evidence that "probiotics" containing *Lactobacillus* can be ameliorative in breast-fed infants with colic. For formula-fed infants, some bottles are marketed to reduce gas intake with feeding, the evidence for which is weak, but there is no harm in trying.

It is quite common for a medical diagnosis of gastrointestinal reflux to be made by pediatricians asked to evaluate an otherwise healthy but fussy baby. Most all babies spit up and experience reflux (acid coming up from the stomach) from time to time. Only in the rarest of cases does reflux cause enough inflammation of the esophagus (the feeding tube) to allow for that to be a plausible explanation for a colicky infant. (Such a diagnosis would often require more-invasive testing including endoscopy and a pH probe.) The all-too-common prescribing of reflux medications for colicky infants is not evidence based and, moreover, brings with it potential side effects. Parents would be well advised to ask their pediatrician for other suggestions to treat colic.

What should I expect at my baby's routine visits with my pediatrician at this age?

In the pediatrics profession, we refer to routine patient visits as well-baby care. These were some of my favorite appointments. Who else has a job that allows them to hold a baby in their hands and call it work?

A lot is going on at these visits. We reassure the parents (and ourselves) that the baby is growing and developing normally. We give "anticipatory guidance"—advice and education about what to expect over the next several months until the next routine visit. We take every question as a chance to build confidence in the parents' own abilities and solidify a relationship of trust that will endure over the next 18-22 years. And last, like Dr. House of network TV fame, we must have a sixth sense about whether, just below the surface, there are problems that are not being mentioned by the parents. Issues with attachment, postpartum blues, domestic violence, substance abuse, grandparents' not respecting boundaries, vulnerable child syndrome, and finances are just some of the concerns that can make for an unhealthy environment for a new baby or a young adult. Most pediatricians will use questionnaires or ask directly about these issues. Do not be offended by such questions and be as honest with your answers as possible. It is the only way your physician can be of help.

Most parents are very interested in growth curves and their infant's percentiles. We measure three areas of growth at this age—head circumference, weight, and length, with length being the least accurate. Eventually, your child will be able to stand, and their height can be measured more accurately.

Unless the baby was premature and is experiencing catch-up growth, your pediatrician is looking for steady growth in all three of these areas. Head circumference can normally be a different percentile than weight and length. Some babies have larger heads on smaller bodies or smaller heads on larger bodies. This is genetically determined, so do not be surprised if your pediatrician wants to measure your head size or ask what size hat your spouse wears. (Fun fact: when you multiply your hat size by *pi*, you get your head circumference in inches.) Steady increases in head circumference along a consistent percentile, coupled with normal acquisition of new developmental skills, allow us all to feel good about the baby's neurologic development. If growth of the head is too fast or too slow, some investigation may be necessary.

The child's length and weight percentiles are more likely to match up and remain steady over time. These are also genetic but do not, at this age, predict adult size. Adult stature can be more accurately predicted when looking at growth curves after puberty begins. Sometimes, breastfed babies get a little heavier when their mothers produce more hindmilk (milk with higher fat content), but these babies usually slim down when weaned.

Some babies will "channel" up or down several percentiles around 4-7 months, but then grow steadily thereafter. Your pediatrician will reassure you, if this occurs, that it is normal. However, poor growth, or "failure to thrive" (FTT), can be the first clue to a medical problem. Fortunately, FTT is a rare event.

Normal development will usually be assessed by questionnaires and observation during the routine exam. Most questionnaires, such as the traditional Denver Developmental Screening Test or newer ones such as Ages and Stages, will measure the acquisition of language, gross and fine motor, social, and problem-solving skills. While these surveys can identify strengths and weaknesses, keep in mind they are only a snapshot in time. It is the progression of skills, or lack of progression, that provides us with clues that normal development is, or is not, taking place. Again, slower areas can be genetic, especially with language and motor development. For example, if you, your spouse, or your child's sibling was a late walker or talker, your child might be late as well. If there are areas of concern, your physician will provide you with specific activities to work on with your child. However, if delays become significant, additional testing or a visit to a pediatric neurologist may be called for.

These visits are also a good time to bring in a list of questions, as your pediatrician will appreciate your being organized about your concerns. Ultimately, this will lead to a better visit, a more efficient use of everyone's time, and a building of trust and mutual respect.

Probably the most important thing you should expect at your baby's visit with the pediatrician is a supportive and safe environment. Hopefully, you took the time to interview several pediatricians before having your first child. Your pediatrician should be a good listener, well informed about the basic science of pediatrics, and always willing to discuss any and all of your concerns. There should be times when your pediatrician will offer praise for your good parenting, but your pediatrician should not be afraid to discuss concerns about parenting efforts that may potentially be problematic for you and your child.

Feeding an infant

Again, this book is not intended as an exhaustive resource about pediatric medicine, including feeding a baby; even so, it's worth mentioning an excellent reference on this, and many other, topics, namely, the American Academy of Pediatrics guide, *Caring for Your Baby and Young Child—Birth to Age 5* (There are additional books in the series on childhood and adolescence including *Your Baby's First Year* a must-have addition to a well-stocked diaper bag).

The decision on whether to breast or bottle feed your baby is up to you. Breastfeeding exclusively is the recommendation of most all pediatricians, including myself, but never against the mother's true preference. Even if you are in doubt about nursing your baby, I would suggest trying breastfeeding. I say this knowing that breastfeeding is a lot of work, especially in the first month when mothers need all the support possible. However, taking into account the immunity breastfeeding imparts, the mother-baby attachment that occurs, and the convenience that eschewing the bottle brings, overcoming your doubts about nursing are likely worth it.

But some parents do choose to formula feed their infants, and the infants do just fine. My language here is important. Some *parents*. It is a decision for couples to make together (with ties going to the mother; after all, she'll be doing the work).

In any event, the avoidance of solid foods through age six months is important. Contrary to some views, the early introduction of solid foods does not result in improving the chance of a baby's sleeping thought the night. When introducing solids, it's important to take your time. Every baby is different, but it will likely take a few days for most babies to warm up to these new tastes and textures. Feeding should be pleasurable for both the baby and the parent. There is no "right" way to introduce solid foods, though most pediatricians advise starting with cereal before introducing vegetables, fruits, and meats. Talk to your pediatrician for advice as some pediatricians prefer that babies receive meats before other solids as it has a higher iron content. Supplemental iron vitamins may be recommended for exclusively breast-fed infants at 4 months of age until iron containing solids like cereal and meats are started.

The only other point I would like to make is about food allergy and tolerance. Tolerance is a medical term suggesting that when infants are exposed through feedings to highly allergenic foods early in life, they may be protected from developing food allergies. In recent years, the scientific community has begun to believe that there would be lower rates of food allergy if infants were fed certain foods earlier in life. This would mark a dramatic change from the advice pediatricians have been giving for years. Studies from Israel show that peanut allergies in that country are less common than in the U.S. and note that Israelis introduce peanut products to babies early in life. If your child has severe eczema, has shown allergy to certain foods (usually eggs), or has a sibling with a food allergy, it is best to discuss with you doctor whether allergy testing should take place before introducing peanuts or other highly allergic foods (cow's milk, soy products, shellfish) to their diet. However, if such allergies are not present, peanuts can be introduced at 6-7 months by mixing two teaspoons of peanut butter with enough warm water to make a paste or by buying a commercially available peanut butter-flavored snack such as Bamba. Pediatricians still advise waiting several days between trying new foods and looking for an allergic reaction such as a rash (hives) or difficulty breathing.

Grandparents

Though my target audience for this book is parents, I would like to make some observations about "grandparenting" in hope that you will share them with your parents. Several years ago, my wife and I experienced that eagerly-anticipated event for the first time. Now I have three beautiful grandchildren and a fourth on the way. A new baby means more family for the grandparents. People have probably told you that being a grandparent is better than being a parent. You get to play with the child but can give them back when you want. Is it really that simple? What about those "rules" about grandparenting that you ought to abide by? Let's address those first, then discuss the opportunities. The following list appears on grandparents.com as the "7 Unbreakable Laws of Grandparenting" though I have changed the wording somewhat. I have also added an eighth "law."

1. Do not give advice unless asked. This is pretty obvious. New parents often receive a constant stream of unsolicited advice from relatives, friends, strangers at the grocery store, you name it. I tell parents to inform their own parents (the grandparents) that it is now the parents' turn to make the best decisions they can for their child. (By the way, when is it ever a good idea to give unsolicited advice to anyone about anything? Just saying.) This is not to suggest you will never have a chance to weigh in on your children's parenting methods. They are now young adults and have probably called for advice about money, a leaky faucet, or an employment interview. Now facing the most important job of their lives, raising their child, they will probably be calling for advice frequently. That will be the best time to give it.

2. You will feel your grandchild is "yours," but they are not. This is the toughest one in my opinion because it's TRUE. If your relationship with your grandchild's parents is based on trust (not money, help provided, obligation, or guilt), there will be many opportunities to nurture your grandchild in a healthy manner.

3. Follow the parents' rules. When you are babysitting, you may find yourself questioning the parents' instructions for care. This is particularly true when the instructions (or technologies used) are different from when your last child was born. Remember that nobody knows your grandchild better than their parents. Sure, information on child rearing keeps changing, but let mom and dad put their trust in the advice of their pediatrician and reliable websites. Three websites that are reliable are aap.org., immunize. org., and babycenter.com.

4. Accept your role. I would not worry about this one. You are a relief pitcher. I say, what's so bad about that? Bruce Sutter and Mariano Rivera were, and they're in the Hall of Fame. I had families in my practice where the "relief" role for the grandparents was vital in terms of time committed to such duties as daily daycare or babysitting to give their kids a night out. Whatever the role, embrace it.

5. It is not a competition. Here, we are talking about competing with the other set of grandparents. The grandchild can only be better off if more people love them. Sharing a grandchild has allowed my wife and me to have another couple that we consider best friends.

6. Respect boundaries. Being a grandparent can create boundary issues. My rule of thumb is whether I would have wanted my own parents to be involved in a particular activity, decision, or life event of my own children. This rule means there are some things and events I should never miss and other times when I should choose not to be involved.

7. Let go of all expectations. This a good suggestion in life, but especially in your closest relationships. Most of us have experiences where people or life circumstances do not meet our expectations. Being a grandparent is similar. It has highs and lows. It will be unpredictable. It will change you, and if you have the right attitude, those changes can be for the better whatever the circumstances.

8. Praise good parenting efforts and behaviors. Your child and their spouse will do a lot of things well when it comes to caring for their new baby, yet may have little confidence in their abilities with this important responsibility. Praise is invaluable. Do not be shy about giving it.

Following these rules to the best of your ability should result in your child's trusting you with their child. Isn't that a strange concept?

We will discuss trust further in our adolescent section, but for now, suffice to say that trusting your adolescent child can be a challenge at times. They do not always follow "the rules." Similarly, grandparents do not always follow all the rules, and now we have turned the tables. We now wish to have our children's trust with their most valued "possession." Once this trust is established, we can watch our grandchildren develop, see the world again through a child's eyes, provide encouragement and support to both our grandchildren and their parents, and maybe be allowed to have our grandchildren spend the night so that we are the first ones to hold them when they wake up in the morning smiling in their crib.

Fatherhood

What an opportunity we all have when a child is added to our family! I contemplated writing about fatherhood to urge fathers to "lean in" and be present every step of the way in their child's upbringing. Then I realized I wanted the advice in this book to be directed to parents from a gender-neutral perspective. As it was, some of the families I cared for had same-sex parents and others were single parents. In rare situations, I saw fathers more often than mothers. (What a delight it was seeing a male firefighter parent bring his children in for visits.) Even so, it seems sensible to address fatherhood in a book about child rearing.

The issues of parental presence and making the best-informed decisions for your child should be at the forefront of both parents' minds. Though asking fathers to be more involved for the sake of their children and themselves should not be necessary, seeing only the mother in the office was still the most common situation during my years in practice. Not only was the mother often the only parent in the office, she seemed to carry the primary responsibility for the child's wellbeing as well.

An interesting discussion about this issue of responsibility occurred in *Money* magazine between Lisa Wade (Dec. 29, 2016) and Josh Levs (Jan. 5, 2017). Their articles carried similar titles—"The Invisible Workload that Drags Women Down" and "The Invisible Workload that Drags Men Down, Too." Ms. Wade's article made reference to what I often saw, that women do more of the intellectual, mental, and emotional work of raising children, work that produces excessive worry for them. Mr. Levs' article spoke of men not letting on about how anxious and stressed they feel in the traditional role as provider. I saw this also at times.

Fatherhood is a big job. And it's not just in the trying and tiring time of infancy but all the way through, up to and including adolescence. It works best when the "workload," and I'm not talking about just the chores around the house, is shared. If this sharing was not modeled in your own childhood, it may not come naturally. I think I speak for all pediatricians in inviting parents to participate fully and to strive for a healthy balance in making parenting work for both partners. As always, communication is the key.

Pet peeves, or what was most challenging during this period of development

Each section of this book will discuss a pet peeve I have about the age group under discussion. Perhaps pet peeve is too strong an expression, but I do want your attention. These are areas of opportunity where a lot can be at stake. Usually, I will refer to behaviors of parents, but I will also try to look at my own abilities and skills to help parents in these situations. I hope you find these areas helpful, and my comments not too judgmental.

For infants, a major pet peeve was seeing parents walking their infant in a stroller or sitting in the park with their baby BUT ON THEIR CELL PHONE. Perhaps it was an emergency call. I think we have all seen this too often for that to be a reasonable explanation. Rather, I suspect most young parents feel compelled to stay perpetually in contact with work and friends. I remember seeing a father in my waiting room with his infant strapped to his body in a carrier. He was busy showing the six-month-old the different fish in our water tank. "See the blue fish swimming?" he said. "It looks like Dory." What a contrast to the parents on their cell phones.

Children learn about the world from intimate contact with their parents—eye-to-eye contact, touch, and vocalization. Parental presence will be a theme in the book as we move forward. Not being "present" during the adolescence years can be a catastrophic error. One cannot suddenly become present during that time period. Infancy is the starting line though I am not sure anyone truly ever finishes.

So, start now. Put the phone down and talk to your baby, smile at your baby, and echo their verbal efforts back to them. Watch a grandparent. This is what they do. Perhaps they are making up for their own omissions in the past.

Chapter 3

TODDLER LIFE

It is 8 o'clock and bedtime for my kids. Their baths have been completed and their teeth have been brushed. The kids are now almost two and four. My wife and I are ready to again read "Goodnight Moon" and then have some peace, quiet, and the rest of the evening to ourselves.

On your mark, get set, go! Yes, your baby is now on the move, and you will be also. This term, toddler, is derived from the verb toddle—an unsteady gait that we all can recognize with a smile on our faces. Toddling and walking are motor skills, but much is also happening developmentally at this age as children acquire language, develop intellect, express emotions, and demonstrate social skills. In this chapter I would like to explore some of the challenges, changes, and issues of toddler life including separation, autonomy, self-esteem, discipline, limit setting, the beginnings of sexuality and gender identification, parenting styles including helicopter parenting, safety, and diet. Whew! I'm already tired. These issues may manifest themselves to the pediatrician as problems with sleep, toilet training, willful behavior, or in a host of different ways. A great reference here is the classic book by perhaps America's most famous pediatrician, T. Berry Brazelton, *Touchpoints—Birth to Three.*

Safety

Mobility and curiosity make toddlers more at risk than infants for injury and bring safety issues to the forefront. I remember receiving a phone call one day just after the office had closed. The mother was frantic. Her three-year-old child had just eaten a goldfish while in the car. This was a new one for me. Imagine how surprised I was to learn that this "goldfish" was a cracker and had been glued to the boy's artwork from pre-school.

Another memorable phone call was from a mother who indicated that her child had swallowed a dime. He was not having any breathing problems and was able to swallow a piece of bread I asked her to give him. When she inquired if she needed to call me back when she saw the dime in his bowel movement over the next day or so, I replied to only call back if she saw a nickel and 5 pennies come out.

Kids put things in their mouths. Choking is the most common cause of cardiopulmonary arrest in young children. Lessons in how to properly aid a choking child through the use of the Heimlich maneuver or the modified Heimlich maneuver are available at your local hospital or American Red Cross location (children less than one year of age would receive back blows between the shoulder blades with the child placed prone along your forearm). Though it is probably not beyond the expertise of your pediatrician or their staff to teach this in the office, complete CPR training is best learned elsewhere. Only perform the Heimlich or modified Heimlich maneuver if the child is not moving air effectively. A "choking child" still coughing or talking is fine and needs no help. Avoiding common foods that represent choking hazards, including popcorn, peanuts, and hard candies, is key. Hot dogs and grapes should be quartered until around age four. Coins can be a problem. Quarters often get stuck at the very top of the esophagus and may need to be removed at the hospital. Another serious potential choking hazard is button batteries. Ingesting these can lead to erosive injury of the esophagus and will require immediate medical attention and usually surgical removal. The same is true when magnets are ingested.

Unintentional injuries, especially car accidents, remain the greatest cause of death throughout the pediatric years. Car safety recommendations are pretty straightforward. It is recommended until two years of age that children be placed in a rear-facing infant or convertible car seat. Young children, who lack adequate head control, need to face the rear to avoid serious neck injuries that can result from a sudden stop. And do not worry about their legs being too long and cramped. Neck protection is more important. Most toddlers will outgrow infant-only seats and need to be placed in a convertible or a forward-facing seat with a harness when their weight or height exceeds the limits set by the manufacturer. At that time, children can ride in booster seats. It is important to follow weight recommendations for any seat you purchase. A seat belt will not properly fit children until they are 4-feet, 9-inches tall, and children should not ride in the front seat until age 13 because of potential neck injury from air bags. Finally, will you, the parent, be attentive? Your responsibility to your child makes it imperative not to text or use your cellphone while driving and not to drive under the influence of alcohol or drugs.

Falls are part of life, but falls down the stairs or from a crib can result in significant injury. Toddlers will require a baby-proofed home with stairway gates and attention to cords, sharp-edged furniture, safe storage of cleaning products, and recognition of the hidden dangers in the kitchen, bathroom, and garage. Until your child has outgrown their crib, very few objects, if any, should be placed there with your child. A small lovie for comfort should be enough. There is no set time that children will outgrow their crib, but they should be placed in a toddler bed or simply a mattress on the floor at the first sign that they might crawl out and injure themselves. This transition can be made easier for your child by having a "big boy" or "big girl" party complete with balloons and perhaps a cake. If you plan to use this crib for a new sibling that is coming soon, try to make this change at least several weeks before the new arrival, and though I would not dismantle the crib, I would leave it bare (without blankets) and less appealing to the child who has outgrown it.

Diet

A mother called me one day to discuss a problem she was having with her child at mealtime. It was a difficult conversation for us as English was not this mother's primary language. Ultimately, I asked her to bring the child in the next day to have lunch with me. She set up his high chair in the middle of the room, and after he refused her attempts to feed him, she removed him from the chair and chased him around the room with a spoon while he played. At that point, the mother and I hit the pause button and proceeded to have a conversation. I told her it was time for her son to control his own food intake and that he might not eat for a few days but it would only take a day or two until he would enjoy feeding himself and everyone would be happier. When I called back several days later, the problem had been solved.

We need to provide healthy choices to toddlers and let them control their own food intake, even if it means they do not eat three meals a day or every day of the week. Some days will be better than others. Their intake is usually lowest at dinner when they are tired and winding down and have what doctors call physiologic anorexia. Since this is often the only meal of the day the entire family shares, it can produce unnecessary concern and occasionally leads to parental pressure to finish dinner, and even threats. I have found that both children and their parents usually feel better when their portion size is small enough that they may actually finish their dinner and make "all gone." Even taking into account such erratic eating habits by their toddler, many parents are surprised to learn how slow normal weight gain is during these years as children add only 4-8 pounds per year.

Another problem, if you are not careful, will be finding yourself becoming a short-order cook. The family might have a standard meal and you will prepare a PBJ sandwich or mac and cheese for the little one. That is not necessary. Studies have shown that parents will often stop offering a particular food after the child refuses it five times. However, the same studies show that when the food is repeatedly offered up to 15 times, the child will accept it or as my grandson says—"you get what you get and you don't throw a fit". It can help, when planning dinner, to always have at least one item your child definitely likes.

So, what are the basic rules for a healthy toddler diet?

1. Ensuring they drink plenty of milk, which provides calcium. This should be whole milk from 1-2 years of age (fat is still needed for brain growth) and low-fat milk from age two up. Whether whole or low-fat, the quantity of milk a child this age consumes should be 16-24 ounces a day. Water can be offered if after drinking this amount the child remains thirsty. Juice and other sugar-sweetened beverages may add unnecessary calories, contribute to cavities, and cause diarrhea from the consumption of too much sugar.

31

2. Being picky is normal for a child, but you can offer foods in different ways until you find something your child will like. A carrot can be eaten raw with a dip, steamed, or mashed for example.

3. Offer meals with protein, fruits, vegetables and grains. Visit myfoodplate.gov for additional information on healthy eating. When older and attending school, your child, it can be hoped, will receive nutritional lessons and information in which they learn about these foods—not just about their health benefits, but about how they are grown, smell, and can be prepared. Children are more likely to try different foods if they are "interested" in them than if told they are "good for you."

4. Eat with your toddler. Talk to your toddler while they eat. Make the table a happy place. Try to avoid negotiations about how much they eat at a given meal. If your child has eaten poorly, they will make it up at the next meal.

Some toddlers do start to gain excessive weight, putting them at risk for adult obesity. And remember, toddlers learn from what they see adults do. Preventing the development of obesity through good family choices around food and exercise is much easier than dealing with children when already at an unhealthy weight with the attendant side effects on their physical and psychological health (including, for example, being bullied).

Perhaps you have heard of the 7-5-2-1-0 program. Follow its guidelines if possible:

- 7, eat breakfast seven days a week
- 5 or more servings of fruits and vegetables (a serving being the size of the child's hand)
- 2 hours or less of recreational screen time (none before age two and off- limits in the bedroom or at the dinner table)
- 1 hour or more of physical activity
- 0 sugary drinks (and more water)

Becoming independent

Part of my routine visits with one-year-olds and their parents was to discuss autonomy, as the self-esteem of acting and thinking on one's own is the main work for children at this age. Though evolutionary biology was my major in college, one of my favorite courses was Psychology 101, and perhaps my favorite psychologist was Erik Erikson. He described eight stages of psychosocial development that occur from infancy to adulthood, with the toddler stage marked by children discovering their independence. Erikson called this stage Will: Autonomy versus Shame and Doubt. When this exploration and assertion of independence are encouraged, children develop self-confidence. Alternatively, when they are not supported, or are overly controlled, a child may develop feelings of inadequacy.

You might find yourself cooking dinner and wondering where your one-year-old has disappeared to. A month ago, they would be somewhere around your ankles. Now . . . are they somewhere nearby? And are they safe? Autonomy does bring with it some parental anxiety, but isn't it fun to watch your child grow up and become their own person?

The terrible twos and threes are primarily about children wishing to do things for themselves and developing competence. I remember when my three-year-old grandson was over, and I tried to help him put on his shoes. He told me, "PawPaw, I can do it myself." This made me smile and glad I had not heard, "I'm too little to do it right." Puzzles that once required assistance to be completed can be done alone—most children can toilet train themselves, and self-dressing frees up time for other aspects of child rearing such as reading another book to your child or taking a walk together.

Dr. Brazelton describes three stages of toddler self-discipline that, when parents and teachers respond properly, result in good social skills and healthy emotional development. First, the toddler tests limits. Second, they look for information from adults as to what is and what is not acceptable. Last, if successfully tested, these limits and behaviors are learned and internalized, allowing the child to move more and more away from their parents. Some parents struggle with consistently setting limits. The inability to do so often sets the stage for behavior problems in toddlers that can often continue all the way into adolescence.

Remember that not all children at this age develop autonomy at the same pace. Each is unique and might be quite different from their peers or older siblings. Even within the individual child, developing these competencies can be erratic—two steps forward and one step back. Be patient. Give them attention and positive reinforcement for their successes and compassion for their setbacks. Children this age need your support as they acquire these new skills—the result will be healthy autonomy, not shame and doubt.

Limit setting

Many of us have struggled with a toddler who seems to run the house, or as I prefer to say, "The inmates are running the asylum." They have temper tantrums, defy parental requests, engage in aggressive behaviors, insist on sleeping with their parents, and may be difficult to toilet train as well. Some of these same children, however, attend daycare or pre-school where they are model children. How is this possible? I usually remind parents that at daycare and pre-school, their caregivers do not love the child and may not even like them (just kidding). The daycare or preschool cannot afford an environment that is not consistent 100% of the time. This is very different from the home where children are loved and where excuses tend to be made for a child's testing behaviors (they're tired; just got over being sick; missed the attention of a parent who was out of town on business.) Parents can come up with a lot of reasons to justify their not being consistent about setting limits. But this is really unfair to the child as they function better in those situations when they know their limits. It may seem that I view parents as the problem. Problem or not, it never helps to say that, and I would usually say to parents in the office that they are the solution in any event.

A classic manner in which a limit-setting problem came into the office masquerading as a medical problem related to sleep routines. Parents would make an appointment thinking their child must have an ear infection because the child wakes at night and is unable to go back to sleep on their own. After a normal exam and further history, it would become clear that the child never fell asleep on their own but stalled and threw tantrums until the parent laid down with them. I remember one family that allowed their child to fall asleep on the living-room sofa each night while the family watched TV. When that child awoke at 3 A.M. each night, parents and child had to go back downstairs to the sofa, turn on the TV, wait for the child to fall back asleep again, and then carry him back to bed. Intellectually, parents know such a behavior has become a habit but they will make excuses for the child rather than make the difficult but necessary decision to adhere to a consistent bedtime routine that does not require them to be in bed or with the child until they fall asleep. Usually before we would develop a plan together, I would ask parents if setting limits was a problem or weakness for them. If they answered that it was, I would tell them that we would consider this an opportunity to build their confidence that limit-setting could be done and applied going forward. Parents would almost always find this approach to be a win-win opportunity.

Raising children is complicated. Each child has their own temperament, and each parent has their own parenting style. It is my experience, however, that even the most difficult and willful children will respond when parental "presence" exists. What is "presence"? It encompasses many things. It includes projecting authority and confidence, being a good role model who is sensitive and respectful, communicating *consistent* limits and providing choices when suitable, recognizing age-appropriate behaviors and giving your child positive re-enforcement for those behaviors while ignoring inconsequential misbehavior. It is a big job and often brings more success when a partner (spouse or significant other) is involved. After your child is in bed for the night, spend a few minutes together to share your successes and to problem solve when things don't go so well. Coach each other, but do not criticize or judge each other.

Here are some additional practical points to consider when dealing with troublesome behavior in your child:

1. Save the lectures for the lecture hall. Research has shown that in most situations verbal explanations and instructions do not effectively change a child's behavior. If you want to be effective, praise positive behavior—CATCH THEM BEING GOOD—and ignore most negative behavior as long as it is not injurious to them or

others. Re-directing your child to an alternative activity can often be a good strategy to avoid a struggle.

2. Assess your family routines. Children respond best when their daily activities occur consistently. Adequate sleep is especially important, so respect naps and bedtimes.

3. Set a good example. Children learn from parents as role models. Our homes must provide warmth and respect for others. It might be a good time to take a deep breath before reacting or you might regret your behavior and the example you are setting.

4. *Don't be afraid to say NO if it is a matter of safety.* Children need to be safe and must learn to live with others. If you are unable to set limits when they are toddlers, good luck when they are in their teens! (As is often said, little people, little problems; big people, bigger problems.)

5. Teach children how to express their feelings. Listen carefully to your child and help them find and use words when angry, frustrated, or disappointed.

6. Give children two choices as often as possible. "Would you like a PBJ or grilled cheese sandwich for lunch?" "It is time for your bath [not negotiable, by the way]; you may choose to play a game with me before or after your bath. Which do you want to do?" If there is no choice in a matter, do not offer one.

7. Ignore unimportant misbehaviors. Any limit setting should be based on real safety issues or on the child's developmental ability to comply with the expected behavior. For example, do not expect a toddler not to swing their legs at the dinner table.

8. Strive to be consistent. Children learn best about trusting parental limits and consequences if there are no surprises. If you say a behavior will have certain consequences, mean it.

Consider contacting your pediatrician if:

1. Your child's behavior is a problem at home AND at daycare or pre-school.

2. Your child's behavior is dangerous to themselves or others.

3. You find yourself increasingly frustrated, and especially if you think you are depressed or might hurt your child when frustrated.

4. You and your spouse do not agree on how to best proceed regarding a given issue or issues.

A recurrent theme of this book will be how addressing many of these struggles when the child is young can help in avoiding disastrous outcomes in adolescence. Each stage of childhood can be seen as an opportunity to find your game as a parent before the stakes get really high. Adolescents out of control can make very serious errors in judgement, and setting limits at those ages will be more difficult if that has not been your pattern of parenting. Remember, children need consistent limits to thrive. As they develop the competence to safely make more decisions, that's the time for you, as parents, to step back and watch.

Behavior problems and behavior modification theory

If I'd had a nickel for every parent who complained about their child's whining, I could have retired at 35 instead of 65. But parents grumbling about their child's whining always gave me the opportunity to cite one of the most well-known Psych 101 labs in college. I would usually start by drawing on the disposable paper that covered my office exam tables. I would draw a box and explain, "This is a Skinner box [developed by psychologist B.F. Skinner] and your child is a rat in the box. Now, every time the rat presses this bar, we are going to turn on a small light and give him a Rice Krispie. After a while, the rat will just go to sleep in the corner. But if we reinforce his behavior *variably,* meaning the reward sometimes comes after two bar presses, or sometimes after five, or sometimes seven, he will press the bar the entire hour."

As parents, we often reinforce undesirable behaviors variably. Children simply wear us down whining for the candy bar at the end of the line in the grocery store or wanting to stay up just five minutes more. You may not have given in yesterday or today, or possibly you did not give in at all, but you did give the negative behavior your attention, perhaps stopping an activity with their sibling or your spouse. Sometimes a child is not seeking an object, but rather, simply, your attention. This action and response can become a vicious cycle without your recognizing it because *variable reinforcement* is very powerful as we saw above with our rat in the Skinner box. When we ignore the behavior consistently, the behavior stops ("extinguishes," in the vernacular). Problem solved.

Behavior modification classically refers to the process of reinforcing the behaviors we like—catch them being good—and ignoring behaviors that are less desirable until they extinguish or disappear. Discipline should be limited to situations that could be injurious to the child or others. Moreover, that discipline can be a slippery slope if it becomes physically or verbally abusive. It can diminish a child's self-esteem and model aggressive behavior, and it rarely teaches a child the very self-control needed to learn from the bad behavior. In his book, *Your Child's Health,* Barton Schmitt suggests the following age-appropriate disciplinary techniques:

Six months to 3 years—Structuring the home environment, distracting, ignoring, verbal and nonverbal disapproval, physically moving or escorting the child from the scene, and temporary time out.

Three to 5 years—Preceding techniques plus logical consequences, restricting places where the child can misbehave. Remember that logical consequences must mean you are going to follow through. I remember threatening my two kids in the back seat of the car that we were not going to go to the Cardinals baseball game if they did not stop fighting. Who was I kidding? The tickets were paid for and we were going in any event.

Five to adolescence—Preceding techniques plus delay of privileges, "I" messages (these are used to express assertiveness and convey your feelings, as opposed to "you" messages, which put the child on the defensive), and negotiations in a family meeting when appropriate. An example of an "I" message might be the following: it scares me (your feelings) when I see you climbing up that tree (what's happening) because the branches are not strong enough to hold you and you could fall (the reason).

I found the concept of time out to be less and less useful over the course of my practice. It should certainly not be used as a form of punishment, as it speaks more to the child about imposing control. Though it might play some role in assisting an upset child to self-quiet, I hesitate to endorse that position, knowing that many parents will expand the use of time out beyond its proper limits. *O.K., let's just say NO to TIME OUT.* In situations where in the past you might have employed time out, teach and guide your child. "When I get upset about certain things, I go outside and read a book to calm myself down," you can say, adding, "Do you want to try that?" If they choose not to, often you can just separate yourself from the situation by going outside yourself.

Temperament

In our section on limit setting, the word temperament appeared. I hesitate to give this topic its own, albeit small, chapter. Why do I waver if temperament can be so critical when setting limits and considering discipline and behavior-modification strategies? After all, aren't all kids unique? And don't we as parents sometimes have different expectations from those of our parenting partner?

I appreciate the concept of temperament and often thought of spending more time to define it for each and every one of my patients but worried about these "labels" becoming self-fulfilling prophecies. We do not wish to label a child as shy or a stutterer. Why, then, label them as clingy, intrusive, demanding, stubborn, resistive, defiant, particular, complaining, angry, selfish, bad mannered, hyperactive, anxious, aggressive or interrupting?

That said, understanding the concept of temperament can come in handy for an exasperated family. *The Difficult Child*, by Stanley Turecki, is a highly regarded book on this topic. What I particularly like about Turecki is that he asks you to study your child (essentially in workbook fashion) and to identify both the types of behaviors the child exhibits that are causing problems and the situations and settings when these behaviors occur. This behavioral profile is then whittled down by both parents' agreeing to a list of the most relevant behaviors to manage (not punish). Just the active attention, energy, and time spent by both parents working together should help parents and child alike. An example might be transitions. Some families have repeated tantrums when a child must stop one activity and then move on to the next. Simply communicating what to expect can make these interactions go smoother. One might use a timer and set it for 5 minutes-----when the alarm goes off it is time to brush your teeth and go to bed or stop playing with your toy and head to grandma's house.

Beginnings of sexuality and gender identification

There are two separate office visits that stand out as I think about sexuality and gender identification. The first visit involved a two-year-old boy. When I asked his mother what concerned her that day, she told me there was "something the matter with his big Joe." I knew she meant his penis, but I teased her briefly indicating that we had not studied "big Joe" in medical school. She had a common concern where the penis retracts into a fat pad, making it seem to disappear. Telling the mother her son would outgrow this over his childhood and showing her pictures in a textbook of other children with this "problem," I was able to reassure her that her son was perfectly normal.

The second visit involved a mother who had brought her thriving two-month-old in for a routine visit. When we were finished, and I asked if she had any additional questions, she mentioned her three-year-old son. He was becoming increasingly interested in playing with what most us would call girl toys and things. The prior evening, when her son heard the garage door go up to announce his father's return home, he became very upset and hurriedly put these toys away knowing that his father disapproved of such play.

The first story simply reflects how difficult it can be for many of us to discuss sex and sexuality. We are all raised differently. I made it a point during toddler-year office visits to use proper terms for male and female genitalia, to explain that it was normal for children of either sex at this age to touch their own genitals (I used the word masturbation), to indicate that children will self-identify as boys or girls, and to make sure parents knew that the office was a safe place to discuss concerns about sexuality. With each occurring developmental stage, I intentionally raised additional topics during office visits so that the table was ultimately set for adolescents and their parents to approach sexuality and sexual decision making in as healthy a way as possible and to see their pediatrician as a resource for any questions.

Possibly having this approach to sexuality in the office allowed the second mother to comfortably ask me what do about her three-year-old who preferred to play with dolls. It was a "bigger" question than most that I was usually asked and offered me an opportunity to guide this family toward an outcome where the child would feel good about himself.

The answer to the mother's question begins with understanding gender, which is both biological (chromosomes) and societal (how society defines sexual roles). When a child's behavior does not match masculine or feminine norms, we call that gender variance. By age two, most children know if they are boys or girls and by age three, they know that boys play with cars and girls play with dolls. As they enter school, children have learned how boys and girls are expected to behave in many social situations.

It is normal for children to have some interest in the activities, toys, and clothes of the opposite sex, and this is most properly viewed as not an all-or-nothing phenomenon. Science would suggest that all of us are somewhere on a continuum (a bell-shaped curve) when it comes to aligning ourselves as being masculine or feminine.

However, identifying with the opposite sex becomes more notable if the child consistently prefers opposite-sex playmates, wishes to wear clothing of the opposite sex, or identifies exclusively with the opposite sex parent—in other words, if the interests become a persistent or pervasive part of the child's daily life. Parenting to steer these children to more appropriate interests for their sex is not likely to be successful and sets the child up for poor self-esteem and shame. Regrettably, when the child is of school age, these behaviors or interests may result in peers excluding them from activities or engaging in bullying.

It is important to remember that a child's gender variance does not predict sexual orientation. Sexual orientation is not important to a young child. It is only as they get older that children become aware of which sex they find attractive and the object of their sexual interests. Gender-variant children may ultimately choose partners of the same sex, opposite sex, or both sexes.

So, what should you do when you have thoughts that your child might be gender variant?

1. Make sure your home is a safe haven. Both parents (and extended family and siblings when possible) need to accept the child and allow them to make choices that make them happy. As with all children, the goal is to enhance their self-esteem. It may be very hard for you to accept these behaviors because of how you were raised, in which case counseling may be helpful to gain an understanding of your emotions. Remember, there is nothing you or your spouse did to make your child gender variant and there is no benefit to assigning fault. There is also no benefit in trying to re-direct your child's interests.

2. Listen to your child. A child needs to know they can say anything to you without being judged. As you listen, validate their feelings and reassure them that there is no one way to be a boy or girl. Whatever you do, do not pressure your child to change. If you do, they will simply hide their feelings and feel ashamed.

3. Encourage your child to engage in activities and play with toys that are consistent with their interests. You cannot willfully change your son's interests by signing him up for soccer or football if he really prefers to take dance classes. Nor can you change a girl's interests by not allowing her to wrestle or play ice hockey and insisting on a cooking class. And always bear in mind that your child may need help in navigating certain social situations where their gender-variant behavior is likely to stand out.

4. Advocate for your child and other children with your school or daycare. Encourage your school to have a curriculum about diversity and social-skill development programs. Classmates can, and should, be taught that bullying is wrong. Your child should know that he or she can go to an adult for help if bullied.

5. Avoid labels. We would not want to label children as stutterers or bedwetters. Nor should we refer to a child's behavior as that of a boy's or a girl's.

Remember, the overarching goal of raising children is for them to have good self-esteem and resilience. Ultimately, they will be more prepared for all they will encounter in life if they think well of themselves and are strong. There is no place for the use of shame or guilt in raising our children successfully.

Toilet-training basics

A four-year-old boy came into my office with a chief complaint of painful bowel movements every third day with blood seen at times. His mother indicated that he had been toilet trained since two and a half years old. Since this was not my first rodeo, I took some additional history, realizing that the statement about the boy's being toilet trained might not be exactly true. In fact, he was successful in learning to urinate in the toilet and had been wearing underwear since two and a half, but only on a couple of occasions had he in fact had a bowel movement while sitting on the toilet. He now seemed to fear the toilet and it became his pattern to hold his stool until his nap or bedtime when he was placed in a pull-up. Whenever I received a history like this one, I usually asked the parent whether they thought they themselves would be constipated after 18 months of holding their bowel movements for 2-3 hours each time they felt the urge to go to the bathroom. Usually this would get the point across.

"Toilet training" would suggest a job for the parent to accomplish, but is really a misnomer. Children are best left to "train" themselves (toilet *learning* in the parlance). There may be pressure and judgment from the daycare center, grandparents, or others about the urgency to complete toilet training in a timely fashion, and though parents will certainly be involved in buying equipment, underwear, and in giving positive reinforcement for a child's efforts, planned attempts to train at an arbitrary point in time are doomed to fail, running the risk of being counterproductive and frustrating for all concerned.

What are the signs of readiness to learn? The first sign of readiness, in my opinion, is that the parents must be willing to quit and wait a while before trying again if training does not occur easily. As far as the child's readiness is concerned, children should have enough language to communicate about the process, be strong enough to pull down their own pants, and be interested in using the toilet. It is useful to keep in mind that most children will achieve bowel before bladder control and girls are typically "trained" successfully at a younger age than boys.

As for equipment, a child toilet is less intimidating than the toilets in our homes, can be taken from room to room, and allows for the child's feet to be placed on the floor so that he or she can push. If you choose to use the household toilet, get a small step stool for the child's feet so that the child can push. They will need some underwear (letting the child pick it out for themselves can be motivating). Seeing which TV and movie characters are on most toddler's underwear from year to year is always fun. (Superheroes apparently still carry the day for boys. Thank goodness Barbie is disappearing and being replaced largely by Disney princesses.)

The child can watch adults and older siblings use the toilet and ask for help, or not, anytime they wish to try to go. If you are a fan of formal positive reinforcement, you and your child can make a simple chart to record their progress and offer a small reward when successful. Rewards work better when they are given out with every successful effort rather than as a "grand prize" when toilet training is completed. Usually that is just too far into the future to be meaningful.

For parents, the watchwords are patience, positive reinforcement, patience, positive reinforcement, patience…. And repeat after me: NO PUNISHMENT.

The placement of a child in underwear, as was the case with our four-year-old boy, was premature. For 18 months, the parents, in a sense, enabled the child to declare himself a big boy and themselves a success. Putting their son back in diapers (though counter intuitive) was a challenge for the parents and the child (usually this advice is not accepted at the first visit), but a short course of stool softeners and allowing their child to pass his stool whenever he needed to (wearing diapers again full-time) resulted in less pain, less holding, and a child who soon started to use the toilet himself. Finally!

Fears

Fears are part of the wild imagination that is part and parcel of life in the toddler years. My own daughter was afraid of fireworks, thunderstorms, and even barking dogs as a toddler. Being afraid of the dark is so common, it might be considered abnormal if a child were not fearful.

As I tackled issues about common childhood fears in my practice, I often referred to Dr. Leo Marvin in the 1991 movie classic, *What About Bob?* starring Bill Murray and Richard Dreyfuss. Dr. Marvin had authored a bestselling book called *Baby Steps* in which patients could work through their fears by breaking them down into smaller pieces (i.e., baby steps).

Imagine a child afraid of thunderstorms. I would advise the parents to buy an ice cream cake and place it in the freezer in anticipation of the next good storm. When the storm rolls in, set up a table and chairs in the garage for a thunderstorm party. There, you can hear and see the storm. You can even go out into the driveway to do a thunderstorm dance. And then come back into the garage and enjoy the ice cream cake.

Not every child will respond to a given solution. Parents can sit down and problem solve together with their pediatrician, but breaking down the fear into smaller components is often useful.

Separation fears are a big part of the toddler years. As we indicated before, children often take two steps forward and one step back. They are starting to enjoy their independence and autonomy from their parents and other caregivers, but remain anxious at times about this separation from people to whom they have a strong emotional attachment. This can be more significant when a child has a stay-at-home parent where separating is not the norm.

Some proven ways to approach separation fears in your child include:

1. Using familiar sitters at night and making sure they arrive prior to your leaving. Do NOT sneak out after putting children to bed as they may wake to someone else and be anxious as a result.
2. Having a picture of their parents in their school cubby to check on if they need to. For parents of a child who cries every day when

dropped off at childcare, remember that the crying usually stops after a few minutes.

3. Using a night light or a stuffed animal for fears of the dark. Do not make the mistake of sleeping with your child as that will simply give you another problem to solve.

So, how did we handle my daughter's fears? My daughter was so afraid of annual fireworks displays that we watched them from 20 city blocks away for a while and then gradually moved closer as she tolerated the loud sounds. As far as the dog-barking problem, we just bought a dog. (For anyone interested, Pippi and, later, Ally, became my daughter's best "friends.")

Playtime

I remember one mother asking at the end of a well-child visit for her two-year-old when she might expect her child to play by himself. She complained of feeling exhausted and never being able to get anything done.

Children need unstructured time. This time will be spent often in a more creative fashion than in the often-choreographed activities of play with a parent. My then-toddler son spent more time with a bowl from a kitchen set and a stick from his hobby horse than with many of his store-bought toys.

Independent play does not mean you will not be nearby or that the child is exposed to injury by not playing safely. It's more about their receiving praise and positive reinforcement. Catch them being good—"I like that castle you're building."

Some parents may find it hard to believe, but too many toys can actually be a distraction for the child. After big events like birthdays or Christmas and similar holidays, put away some toys and bring them out at a later date. Also, simple "toys" with multiple uses are often best. A set of blocks is a good place to start, but even the lid of an empty peanut butter jar or some small pots and pans can lead to creative play just as I found with my son and his stick and bowl.

Do not misunderstand your role. You are an awesome "play toy," engineered to read, smile, hug—and play as well. But just as independent play can be learned, it can also be stifled. Like many challenges in parenthood, decide what you value for your child and be *intentional* about making it become a reality.

Helicopter parents

What is all this talk about "helicopter parents," anyway? Is it a new phenomenon? (Actually, the metaphor was first mentioned in a book by acclaimed child psychologist Haim Ginott in 1969.) Is it just a trendy term to describe over-protective parents? And is it not an overly judgmental term for what most parents strive to do—protect their children and prepare them for success in their growing years and, ultimately, in life?

Helicopter parents, as defined by Wikipedia, are parents "who pay extremely close attention to their child's experiences and problems, particularly at educational institutions. These parents rush to prevent any harm or failure from befalling their children and won't let them learn from their own mistakes, sometimes even contrary to the children's wishes. They are so named because, like helicopters, they hover closely overhead, rarely out of reach of their child."

Though we typically apply this term to those parents who hover over their school- age children, the behavior starts, in my experience, during the toddler years when independent play is so crucial. Such "hyper-present" parents shadow their children and direct their play. As pediatrics is all about preventative care, I found that pointing out this potentially harmful behavior early to parents might at times interrupt what could later be problematic issues in their child's psychological and emotional development.

Many child health experts believe that to raise successful children, parents must allow them to do for themselves what they can do, or at least are capable of doing; to make some of their own decisions; and even to make some mistakes along the way—all the very antithesis of hovering. On its face, this approach seems simple, even self-evident, yet there are factors in society that make it difficult despite a parents' best efforts.

First is the media. The world does appear to be a dangerous place for children—just watch the news or read the paper for "proof." Thus, to many parents, hovering seems necessary to prevent the next injury, illness, or serious harm to the child.

Second is technology. The digital world allows us to "hover," as children now carry cell phones, parents can text children and children can text parents for instant help and reassurance, nurseries are equipped with video cameras, parents have access to a child's test scores at school, and on and on seemingly without end. There is no doubt that technology can be a good thing, but it can also make it easier and more tempting for parents already overly protective of their children to now become even more so.

Third is the tendency toward smaller family size, thus giving parents more time to spend with any one child. Often this degree of attention makes a parent so invested psychologically with their offspring that they are unable to step back and allow their child at times to learn from failure. The effects of small family size can be compounded when grandparents (from the baby-boomer generation) are so close to their children (now millennial parents) that these new parents feel judged if they're not protecting their children enough or not having them participate in enough activities. This leads to more hovering, and potentially, feelings of parent-guilt.

In addition to these associative societal factors, parents may hover because of an underlying anxiety disorder that has been diagnosed by a physician or psychotherapist. Though medication and counseling are often helpful in treating this disorder, some parents reject the diagnosis and go untreated.

So, what's a parent to do? These days it seems that some parents feel so responsible for who their child will become that they try to control the process as much as possible. Yet real growing up must involve allowing children to separate and do much of their blossoming on their own.

Here is a list of Do's to make interactions with your child smoother:

1. Stand back a bit and give your child breathing room. Let them fail at times, even if it hurts you, the parent, a little. Allow your child to do more for themselves and only interfere when something is truly dangerous or the child is not developmentally capable of making certain decisions. Ask your spouse or partner for help by observing each other's efforts in this area. Their (and your) feedback can be invaluable.

2. Develop self-awareness. Having a clear understanding of your own personality, how you were raised, your values, your fears, and your strengths and weaknesses will allow you to make changes in your child-rearing practices if you feel changes are necessary.

3. Place limits on the role of media in your home and be a good role model when it comes to setting limits on the use of technology and digital devices.

4. If you believe you have an anxiety disorder, ask for help from your physician, but also inform your pediatrician. The pediatrician can work with you so that you do not raise your child "vulnerably." Children raised vulnerably may lack the very self-esteem you wanted them to have in the first place.

For all parents, but especially those who choose to have a smaller family, try not to hover. If you have yet to decide how large a family you wish to have, remember, there are few things in life that we can have more of that will provide the satisfaction of children—and remember, too, that sometimes, perhaps paradoxically, less attention paid to any one child may help them in the long run to be more self-sufficient and successful.

Autism and autism spectrum disorders

In our last chapter, we discussed what you can expect at your routine visits with the doctor. Your doctor will measure and weigh your child and either ask you questions about their development or have you to fill out a standardized form. After noting that growth and development have occurred normally, all parties are most of the way toward feeling good about the visit.

However, sometimes development is delayed and needs to be assessed. Development can be delayed in any one of multiple areas including fine motor skills, gross motor skills, language, social, or problem solving. While I always believed in my practice that any parent with a concern about their child's development should be taken seriously, I often found that a child, though slower to acquire a new skill than a sibling or a neighbor's child, had development skills that were well within the normal range.

A diagnosis of a developmental delay is made by your pediatrician based on strict guidelines. A delay in a single area such as gross motor skills (late walker) or language (late talker) often resolves itself without the need for therapy and can run in the family (that is, be hereditary). Other delays, when significant, may need to be addressed with physical, occupational, or language therapies.

Autism should be suspected when delays occur in both the areas of language and social development. Autistic children may also exhibit repetitive (known as stereotypic) behaviors such as hand flapping and repeating words, or restrictive behaviors such as lining up their toys. Usually an autism diagnosis is considered between 12 and 24 months of age. Your pediatrician will use a screening tool called the MCHAT at both your 18 and 24-month well child visits. Do not feel foolish about requesting this screening test from your doctor if it was not performed, as early intervention is critical. Most pediatricians will refer your child to a pediatric neurologist or a developmental-behavioral pediatrician for examination and additional testing to rule out other causes for these developmental delays. Ultimately, the diagnosis of autism or autism spectrum disorder is made clinically since there are no blood tests or imaging studies of the brain that are specific to the diagnosis.

A couple of other points:

1. Autism is not caused by vaccines (media.chop.edu/data/files/pdfs/vaccine-education-center-autism.pdf).
2. Autism appears to have some genetic basis though additional factors are likely at work as well.
3. Autistic children are not intellectually challenged. They are different, not disabled. In fact, about 10% are savants with extraordinary intellectual skills. Like all children, they have strengths as well as weaknesses. Some of these strengths can be a source of self-confidence and, later, job success in adulthood.
4. The sooner a diagnosis is made, the better. Applied behavioral analysis (ABA) therapy can bring about meaningful improvement in the ability of autism spectrum children to learn by using behavioral interventions to address joint attention issues (social communication using gestures and gaze), symbolic play (pretend play), engagement,

and regulation of emotion. Many states have laws which mandate that insurers cover the costs of this type of therapy. For more information, see this website: autismspeaks.org/what-autism/ treatment/applied-behavior-analysis-aba.

5. Autism is best referred to as a "spectrum" disorder, a designation that describes a wide range of symptoms, skills, and levels of (dis) ability under a single term. It is important that the diagnostic label of autism does not lead to assumptions about a given child or a failure to see them as unique individuals, as no two autistic children are the same.

An excellent book about autism for children to read is *Noah Chases the Wind,* by Michelle Worthington. A book to read or a play for adults to catch is *The Curious Incident of the Dog in the Night-Time,* by Mark Haddon.

Antibiotic Use

I mentioned in my introduction that our conversation would be less about diseases and their treatment and more about parenting challenges. But just as in the last chapter when we discussed jaundice, I believe that a few things ought to be said about antibiotics that may take us somewhere more meaningful.

Toddlers will catch infections. I once attended a conference where both pediatricians and internists were present. The speaker made a very important point that pediatricians know all too well, but might have escaped some of the internists in the room. He said, "children are sticky". They are full of secretions and freely share them, despite best efforts of hand hygiene.

The majority of the infections a pediatrician will see on a given day are "colds" or what doctors call Upper Respiratory Infections (URIs). These are usually caused by viruses and will run their own course. Occasionally, they will lead to a secondary bacterial infection like an ear or sinus infection, and even then, they may, or may not, require treatment with an antibiotic. Other pediatric infections more clearly require treatment with an antibiotic like strep throat, urinary tract infections, and most cases of pneumonia.

So, what are the meaningful issues here I wished to discuss? First is antibiotic resistance---most have read about superbugs and the fear that bacteria continue to outsmart our medications. This is a real problem now and will likely become an even bigger problem in the future. Therefore, your pediatrician has been trained to use antibiotics judiciously (https:// www.cdc.gov/getsmart/community/for-hcp/outpatient-hcp/pediatric-treatment-rec.html). This often means no antibiotics at all but "watchful waiting" for additional worrisome symptoms. It might mean shorter courses of medication and using the most specific or narrowest spectrum medication to treat the likely offending bacteria.

Unfortunately, several things conspire to make doing the right thing difficult. The biggest is expectations. Many parents have similar symptoms to their child and simply call their doctor and receive an antibiotic prescription over the phone for what was likely a viral infection anyway. They do not understand why their child does not need the same treatment. Additionally, sometimes grandparents apply pressure, not understanding why the pediatrician is not prescribing a medication despite the child's being ill. They might even ask you "How old is your pediatrician?" assuming they are inexperienced and do not know any better. Finally, even the most up to date recommendations are in flux and sometimes parents, and even physicians, must admit that it is not always a straightforward decision to prescribe or withhold antibiotics.

This gets us to the concept of shared medical decision making. This involves talking about the choices---there are almost always choices. This is where your physician needs to share high quality clinical information and explore what you already know about the condition under consideration and what misinformation you might be considering as well. Together, a decision can be reached that is informed. And when this decision is made together, compliance and follow-up improve. Some parents shy away from this type of participation feeling intimidated or afraid to express their preferences and views. Others wish to take over and disregard the advice of their physician altogether. Ultimately, good communication about the child's best interests should rule the day.

Pet peeves, or what was most challenging during this period of development

As children get older, each opportunity to become a savvy parent becomes more important. Some parents of toddlers begin to develop a parenting "style" that can lead to problems down the road. The challenge that stood out most for me at this stage of development was working with helpless parents (Morris Green 1997). Helpless parents were unable or unwilling to follow through to correct behavior issues even when they and I, as a team, developed reasonable solutions together. There were always excuses. Perhaps "pet peeve" is a misnomer, but it was often very hard to "fix" behavioral problems and help certain families. Maybe "frustrations" would be a more apt label.

Do not misunderstand: I had empathy for all my patients, for this group even more perhaps than for others, as they were often struggling to deal with stresses elsewhere in their lives as well. Sometimes it was their marriage, or money, or work, or all three. Perhaps there was untreated anxiety or depression or substance abuse. Most of the time it seemed more about being so busy with the pace of life that giving in to the child was a "quicker fix" than doing what they knew intellectually to be a better choice.

I suppose these patients represented such a great challenge because my training prepared me more for diagnosing and treating infections, rashes, and broken bones than emotional and psychosocial problems.

Why bring this up at all? If you have a toddler and continue to struggle with sleep issues, tantrums, and setting reasonable limits on behavior, open up to your pediatrician as honestly as possible about what lies below the surface. You and your physician can work together to develop reasonable solutions to these commonplace problems but only after, as a team, you get to the heart of the matter. It may simply be that setting limits is truly a weak link in your parenting arsenal. If that is the case, it is shortsighted not to confront this issue now and prove to yourself that you will be able to change before the stakes become higher in the adolescent years. If it is a matter of an anxiety disorder or stress related to work or home, do not postpone addressing these problems either. No matter what the issue, your child will benefit if it is addressed sooner rather than later.

Chapter 4

EARLY-SCHOOL-AGE CHILDREN

It is the first day of kindergarten and my daughter is anxious but ready. As parents, we are just anxious. We have been reading "Grover Goes to School" for weeks and give her Grover's mother's advice that she is very likeable and will make new friends.

Does your child need to attend pre-school?

Over the years I was often asked about the value of pre-school. Most parents believe pre-school is part of their "pact" with their children that they will provide "everything my child needs" throughout the parents' lives. However, some families find the cost of pre-school prohibitive while others intend to home-school their children for personal reasons.

Whether pre-school and programs such as Head Start are a cost-effective strategy for large populations of our country's children is about politics and policy, a different discussion than the value of the programs to an individual child. Research points to long-term benefits in the form of decreased dropout rates, decreased grade repetition, and fewer teen pregnancies. Short-term benefits for the child may be related more to showing up for kindergarten on day one less anxious about school routines, perhaps being well received by the teacher as "bright," and already having acquired some basic learning skills.

When asked, how did I answer this question in the office? I would tell parents that from a short-term perspective, basic educational skills such as being able to read or write a little will catch up quickly. In terms of lessening anxiety and being ready for the routines of kindergarten, at least six months of pre-school is likely beneficial for all children though not absolutely necessary. I would add that longer periods of time in pre-school may be of additional value if the alternative is an environment with little stimulation.

I suppose the ultimate goal is that children have a love of learning. It must be remembered that this love will not occur simply because a child attends pre-school and, eventually, school itself. It must be part of the fabric of the home as well.

Should my child enroll in a public, private, or parochial school?

This is another question I was often asked. Again, what are your goals and what are your values? Were you and your spouse educated in similar environments as children? Is the decision related to cost, quality of education, class size, role of religion in the curriculum, likelihood of secondary school or college acceptance—something else, or elements of all these?

My most important piece of advice was for parents to identify their values and then interview ALL the schools under consideration. Just as with buying tennis shoes, the more you pay does not necessarily mean you have chosen the right fit for your child. Most home budgets will only allow for public school education but even here you might have a choice between local, charter, and magnet schools. Go see them and talk to other parents in your community that you respect for their opinions.

If your child has learning difficulties and qualifies as learning disabled, under federal law, they must be provided with an individual education plan (IEP). Additional educational services and accommodations are required to be available at your child's public school through the course of the day. If you choose to educate your child at a private or parochial school where individual education services are not offered, these additional learning activities are still available through your public school district's special education program provided after school hours. For some children, this might be too long a day and may need to be factored into your school choice.

Some families choose to homeschool their children. I am neither pro-nor anti-home schooling. If you are well suited to teach your own children, make sure the curriculum you use is properly vetted and that your child has opportunities for socialization outside the home.

Should I hold my child back before starting school?

I was born in June and back in the 1950s it never occurred to parents that they should hold their children out of school to gain maturity or some sort of competitive advantage. In the U.S., there is little uniformity among states governing the age for starting kindergarten, but generally the starting age is five. However, the average starting age is creeping up due to the growing trend of holding kids back. In some schools, a kindergarten child might be 18 months older or younger than a classmate.

What defines readiness, anyway? Some kids at this age can already read and write, sit attentively though a 30-minute story, and follow simple directions. For me, as a doctor, it was more about the latter two skills than the first. Being capable of learning from a behavioral standpoint is the key. The reading and writing will come.

But though "redshirting", a term used in college athletics for freshman who are asked to sit out a year to physically mature, may give kids an academic advantage (studies are actually mixed on this question), it can also have an impact on social issues down the line—such as being more advanced in puberty than their classmates and reaching legal driving age earlier as well. Both of these issues have been reported to be contributors to more behavioral problems in adolescence and, at times, poor academic performance.

So how did I answer this question in the office? There are some children who would benefit from an additional year of behavioral maturity if they do not have an adequate attention span, good gross- and fine-motor skills, and ability to follow directions. I told my patients that their child's pre-school teacher should be able to reassure them that these skills are present. Most schools prior to kindergarten offer pre-testing that will look at these characteristics as well. If you choose to hold a child back a year, it is not enough to just have another year go by. These delayed skills will not simply appear magically with additional time. It must be a year where your child is in an educational environment and their deficiencies are being addressed. If this cannot occur, I would rather they take a shot at kindergarten and repeat it if necessary.

The teacher says my child is struggling in school.

Hardly a week went by in my practice that I did not receive a phone call from a family about their child struggling academically in some fashion. This could have been the result of an undiagnosed learning disability, attention deficit disorder (ADD or ADHD), social problems, emotional problems, or simply being bored.

As with all medical issues in a pediatrician's office, a proper diagnosis should start with a good history, so do not be surprised if your pediatrician's first step is to obtain some information from you as parents and from your child's teacher as well.

There are many standardized forms for gathering this information. I like the Vanderbilt questionnaires (nichq.org/childrens-health/adhd/resources/vanderbilt-assessment-scales) as a starting point to look for classic signs of ADD and ADHD. These questionnaires will also give parents and teachers a chance to provide additional insights about behavioral issues such as an anxiety disorder or ODD (oppositional defiance disorder).

In children and adolescents where my index of suspicion was high that there were emotional issues playing a role, I used the Pediatric Symptom Checklist (PSC) (brightfutures.org/mentalhealth/pdf/professionals/pedsymptonchklst.pdf). The PSC allowed parents to give me a more nuanced description about how their child was coping and functioning emotionally from day to day. If the need for help is indicated, mental health professionals such as child psychologists or psychiatric social workers can work with children with specific needs or diagnoses. School counselors might also be helpful and, at times, can involve your child in social-skills groups when this is the problem issue.

Educational testing, if it has not already been performed by the school, can be requested by parents. Laws in the U.S. mandate that IEPs (Individual

Education Plan) be developed for children with learning disabilities or with medical diagnoses, such as deafness or blindness, that interfere with school learning. Educational testing will measure your child's intelligence and also measure specific skills of brain function needed for learning (oral comprehension, listening comprehension, written expression, basic reading skills and comprehension, basic math skills and reasoning). These are functions that affect how the brain receives, processes, analyzes, and stores information. Each of us is hard wired (brain connections/neurons) to learn with different strengths and weaknesses, but a learning disability is properly diagnosed when there is a statistically significant discrepancy between the child's intellectual ability and their achievement in one or more areas or when a child carries a medical diagnosis which interferes with their educational performance over an extended period of time.

Over my years in practice, many parents feared this "labeling" of their child. Perhaps acceptance would be easier for parents if physicians and educators could consider these designations more as learning differences than disabilities. Differences imply variation whereas disabilities can carry the stigma of being less intelligent, which usually is not true. However, if your child is struggling to learn, you really should welcome the designation of a learning disability/difference (if it truly applies), as it will bring practical help in the form of special educational services including possible accommodations or modifications for your child. Accommodations might include untimed testing, preferential seating in class, verbal rather than written testing, and teacher outlines of lecture material, for example. The accommodations should be specific to the areas of identified weakness. Modifications, on the other hand, will consist of larger changes in the curriculum content and expectations of performance. This LD diagnosis and its treatment will be reviewed and reassessed by the school at regular intervals. Additionally, parents, at any time, can request that this review occur sooner when needed. And remember, some children ultimately outgrow the need for additional services. A useful website to review learning disabilities is ldaaamerica.org.

Part of the evaluation for a child struggling in school will include a thorough physical exam including hearing and vision testing. However, in my experience, rarely will a physical examination uncover abnormal neurological findings that need to be addressed. Though a referral to a child neurologist can be made in these children, it is usually not necessary.

Attention deficit disorder and attention deficit disorder with hyperactivity affect 5-10% of all school-aged children. These diagnoses are associated with much controversy among the general public. Some families strongly reject ADD or ADHD as a possible diagnosis, seeming to fear the prospect of medication. Other families are just the opposite.

Often families asked me if these conditions were over diagnosed. I would answer that they were likely over *and* under diagnosed. The challenge, like most challenges in medicine, is to properly diagnose. Unfortunately, there are no blood tests or brain scans in common use or physical findings on examination to make these diagnoses definitively. To do so, as physicians, we must rely on history alone. This history, when provided by parents and teachers through standardized forms like the Vanderbilt scales mentioned above, must show the problems exist in two or more environments (home, school, activities), have persisted for at least six months, and had onset prior to the age of twelve. What we look for are six of nine symptoms that occur to a significant degree in the areas of inattention and/or hyperactivity/impulsivity. (For more, visit cdc.gov/ncbddd/adhd/diagnosis.)

During some routine visits, parents would tell me that a friend or relative thought their child was hyperactive and needed to be treated with medication. Just being busy does not mean a child has ADHD. Busy children are at risk for more injuries but can often learn and focus appropriately in school environments.

It is rarely useful to make an ADD or ADHD diagnosis before school age though it can be made down to the age of four. In my opinion, starting a child on medications before the age of five or six is to be avoided unless the child is very disruptive to the normal functioning of the household or is creating similar problems at their school. Behavior-management techniques should be tried first and are often effective on their own at this age.

It is beyond the scope of this book to discuss treatment options except to indicate that only medication and behavioral therapy have been shown to be effective in clinical studies (cdc.gov/ncbddd/adhd/guidelines). For those families that are averse to treatment, it is important to remember that as with other diseases, failure to treat can be associated with negative consequences. Just as untreated diabetes can lead to problems with the heart, kidneys, eyes, and other bodily functions, complications of untreated ADD and ADHD can lead to low self-esteem, truancy, and substance abuse.

It does not help in our discussions with parents that when considering a diagnosis of ADD/ADHD and making treatment decisions there are no specific tests to make a "certain" diagnosis of ADD, and that patient history alone guides our decision to treat with "brain-active" medications. As physicians, we are not looking to treat children so they might be better behaved in school (or become zombies, as some parents express with fear). Rather, we are looking to treat children so that they can learn more easily. I suspect few parents would debate the need for their child to take insulin after a diagnosis of diabetes has been made. Likewise, the use of stimulant medications for attention problems should be strongly considered by parents as well. (If side effects occur, including dramatic changes in the personality of the child, these medications should be stopped or changed.) Alternative treatments such as biofeedback training, homeopathic medications, and the Feingold diet do not have the weight of science behind them and should be discouraged. Two good resources for ADD /ADHD include the website chadd.org and the book *Driven to Distraction,* by Edward Hallowell.

Emotional issues such as depression or anxiety can by themselves be the cause of academic struggles. Anxiety, especially, can mimic ADD/ADHD. Both of these conditions must be explored through a detailed history whenever a child is having school difficulties. It is also important to remember that multiple issues can occur in the same child. It is well known that up to one-third of children with an ADD/ADHD diagnosis have simultaneously coexisting (comorbid) disorders such as a learning disability, depression, or anxiety.

Be honest with your physician if your home is in turmoil. Stress in the home can be responsible for academic underachievement. Parents with physical or mental health problems, economic issues like job loss, ongoing substance abuse, or divorce can all create environments resulting in a child's performing poorly in school. It should not require detective work by your physician to bring these issues to the forefront.

Could it be your child is simply gifted and bored? Have you ever met a parent who did not think their child was gifted? Gifted children do exist.

Academically gifted children often have superior verbal, math, and reasoning skills. If not identified and challenged in school with enrichment activities, they can appear disinterested and bored.

Though giftedness must be addressed, it can create problems if undo attention is placed on one gifted child with several siblings in the household. The family's life should not revolve around a single child's giftedness any more than around a single child's disabilities or significant medical problems.

Sibling rivalry

I remember receiving a phone call one day from a mother who was crying. She told me that her daughter had asked her when they were going to take the new baby back to the hospital. And she meant for good!

Many parents have expressed their angst to me about what emotional and psychological harm they were doing to the first child by having another child. My stock comment is they're doing the first born a *favor*. None of us in life will receive the undivided attention and adulation a first child receives from their parents (unless, of course, we ourselves were first children). It is not the way of the world, and a child's learning that sooner rather than later is probably a healthy thing.

Bringing a new baby home can be managed fairly easily. Your older child will probably alternate between loving and ignoring the baby. Some simple suggestions to try to reduce the opportunity for sibling rivalry include making sure your child visits you in the hospital, and if possible, trying to make that first visit without the baby in your arms, at least initially; recording a bedtime story on your cell phone to replay at home while you are still in the hospital with the new baby; having the two children exchange gifts; and wrapping up a few inexpensive items for your older child to open if visitors bring gifts for the baby but forget the older child.

Sibling rivalry can be a real problem and can continue throughout adulthood. Many of us are all too familiar with adults who still play out these dramas. How can you, as caring parents, manage this normal jealousy and competition for your attention, love, and approval? Here are a few ideas:

1. Stay out of the middle. Let the children work it out for themselves and only intervene if you are concerned about physical harm occurring.

2. Do not compare children when talking to them or others.

3. Do not be obsessed with treating them equally. Make it clear to them that you will try to meet their individual needs and that these will be different at times.

4. Modeling good behavior is always important with children. If you do not get along with your own adult siblings and expose your children to fighting and bickering, perhaps there is a way to improve these relationships and be a better role model.

Activities in your community

My son was in first grade at a public school when we learned that many of his peers would be signing up for Tiger Cubs. Tiger Cubs was for boys too young for the Cub Scout program at our school. When we attended the first meeting, the activities described included visiting the fire department and a local McDonald's restaurant. I asked the leader why these seemingly inane activities were chosen, and I was told the kids were too young for real Cub Scout activities. I then suggested to the group, on our way out the door, that maybe we were just rushing our kids.

What is the purpose of getting involved in sports and hobbies at this age? Obviously, there are many benefits to these structured opportunities to learn new skills, meet new friends, get away from Mom or Dad (unless they have volunteered or are truly needed to coach or supervise an activity), and be exposed to additional adult role models. But as illustrated above in my story about Tiger Cubs, one does have to be careful that the activities are good learning experiences and age appropriate.

Team sports allow children to avoid isolation that can result from excessive shyness or a lack of confidence. Moreover, they give kids practice with winning and losing, as resilience is a valuable tool in life. Team sports can also remind kids that every child has something to offer and that each child should be respected equally. The value of teamwork will play a role throughout their education and career. And of course, there is the goal for all of us to get our kids moving and avoid the complications of our increasingly sedentary culture (video gaming and media use are at all-time highs).

Fortunately, during my practice career, girls participating in sports has become the norm. Studies report that higher levels of self-esteem, a healthier body image, and an elevated sense of psychological well-being occur when girls participate in sports. When they continue to participate through high school, additional benefits of improved grades and reduced pregnancy rates are also seen.

Some sports require a great degree of fine-motor coordination and may be frustrating for many children at this age. Steering a child to big-muscle sports such as gymnastics, soccer, dance, and swimming is often a wiser approach than choosing baseball, hockey, golf, or tennis.

A balance of activities can be a good thing also, though over-scheduling can lead to undo stress. Music lessons, often starting with piano, can set in motion a lifetime skill that many of us wish we had. Theater, chess, rock climbing, cheerleading, scouting, martial arts . . . kids have so many choices.

Swimming is among the choices that is, in my opinion, a must. This is not about exercise or becoming proficient enough for serious competitive swimming. It is about safety—period. If you have chosen to have a pool at your home it should have a fence around the entire perimeter (actually, a legal requirement almost everywhere). Access to the pool through the back door of the house can be a safety concern, so you must make sure the door is secured.

Independent play is important and there is only so much time in the day. I hope you started to consider independent play when your child was a toddler. They will need time alone to recharge, use their own imagination, and perhaps even pursue an activity of their own choosing. Watch for signs of being over-scheduled, some of which include always being tired, losing interest in a favored activity, or not wanting to play with a best friend.

Sexuality and sexual play

In our toddler chapter, we began to discuss sexuality and gender identification. I advised parents to use correct terms for genital anatomy, to accept genital stimulation (masturbation) as normal, and to recognize that children this age are exploring the concept of male and female differences. During the pre-school stage, sexual play and sexual interest increase, as do the questions from parents. Here is just a sampling from over the years along with my answers:

- "Is it still O.K. to have my children bathe together? They are five and seven and of different sexes." My answer was probably not.
- "My [12-year-old] son masturbates. When can I expect this to stop?" I told the parent he may never stop but he must do it in private. This response was not well received. I would have given the same answer if the question had been about a female patient.
- "My daughter was sent home from school today for pulling down her pants. She is six years old. Is this normal?" My answer here was that it was probably normal, but that some learning needs to take place.

Sexual play is more the norm than the exception. One example is when kids "get naked" to explore the differences in their bodies. Depending on how a parent was raised or other factors, this can be no big deal or a very big deal indeed.

A study that I found helpful over the years was published in the journal *Pediatrics* in 1991 (and again in 1999) by William N. Friedrich, surveying normative sexual behaviors in Dutch children from the ages of 2-12. When asked questions by a parent such as those above, I would look at the specific behavior and age and, in consultation with Friederich's article, was often able to reassure the parent that a specific behavior was common. (For example, the article suggests that taking down one's own pants in front of another child occurs at this age range in 7.1% of children.) A more disturbing parental inquiry involved a family where the older male sibling (nine years old) made his younger female sibling (five years old) put her mouth on his penis. He had learned this from his 12-year-old cousin at a family birthday party. From Friederich, I discovered, not surprisingly, that this occurred at a frequency of 0.3% among the children studied and, thus, clearly represented a problem for the boy and his family.

So, what is our job as parents?

1. Talk about sexual anatomy with proper names. Answer questions, if asked, about pregnancy, the birth process, and sexual intercourse in line with the child's curiosity and intellectual development, not beyond. When finished, ask: "Does that answer your question?"

2. Teach that interest in your body is normal but that there are rules. When two children of the same age are caught "playing doctor," respond gently. Ask them to put their clothes back on but do not shame them for their activity. Tell them that in the future they are to keep their clothes on when playing together and to never touch someone else's private parts. (You can be specific with the names if you know what was touched.) The next time the two are over together, be close by to supervise their play. Do not forget to notify the other family of what had occurred so that they can speak to their own child as well.

3. Buy a book for learning. For young children, *What's the Big Secret? Talking about Sex with Girls and Boys,* by Laurie Brown; and *Where Did I Come From?* by Peter Mayle are good choices; for early pubertal children, *It's Perfectly Normal: Changing Bodies, Growing Up, Sex, and Sexual Health,* by Robie Harris, is excellent.

4. Have a conversation with your partner and decide on house rules for parents—no co-bathing or showering after your child reaches age five, close the bathroom door when using the toilet or showering, and keep a bathrobe handy to put on when getting out of bed in the morning if you sleep naked. Personal boundaries are part of society and need to be learned at home.

5. For families that have chosen a family bed, be aware that in "primitive" cultures where this is a more common choice, most children show signs of wanting to leave the family bed at around five years of age and should be allowed to do so if you use the family bed in your home.

6. Call your doctor for advice if sexual play has occurred between children of different ages or if the play seems unusual. Also call if your child shows excessive interest in sexual play. And definitely call if you are concerned that your child may have been sexually abused.

The early-school-age years are not the only time you will be discussing sexuality in your home. Addressing sexuality is a big opportunity to give your children knowledge and self-confidence, but because of your upbringing and life experiences, you may be more or less comfortable talking about sex to them than you might like. It is important to develop a plan with your partner and talk to your children together. You are setting the stage for the years ahead. You are modeling respect for the issues under discussion, respect between genders, and ultimately respect for the role of healthy sexual behavior in intimate relationships. You are also creating the expectation for your children that you have the answers to questions about sex. This will encourage them to approach you in the future instead of only getting information from friends, older siblings, the internet, or health teachers. Perhaps most importantly, this will give you a chance to share not just your knowledge, but your values.

Divorce

Why write about divorce in a chapter about early-school-age children? I guess because divorce just seems to happen more when children are this age. Obviously, divorce can occur at any stage of childhood (or adulthood). During the length and breadth of my practice, it seemed at times that divorce was a way of life, and the national statistics seem to bear that out, with 40% of first marriages and 60% of second marriages ending in divorce. The average age of a divorced parent is 30, leaving a lot of young children in divorced households.

If a divorce occurs when the child is an infant, the most important thing you can do for them is to maintain routines and be emotionally available. If you are depressed, seek treatment.

Toddlers and young children are inclined to have "magical thinking" and may blame themselves. They may need to be reassured that they did not do something themselves that resulted in the divorce. They, too, need for routines to be respected. Do not be surprised if they display behavioral regressions such as tantrums or have setbacks in toilet training.

Conversations with a spouse or former spouse often are filled with anger and need to take place away from children or after they are in bed (even then they may be listening). Arrangements need to be made for both parents to see their children with a predictable schedule. Believe it or not, some divorced parents continue to live in the same house. I never saw this work out well.

Early-school-aged children often feel lost and abandoned when their parents choose to divorce. Sometimes they are pressured to choose sides. At this age, kids are capable of expressing their feelings but will likely need to do this independent of both parents—that is, with a professional counselor.

Some kids suffer in other ways when divorce occurs. I often saw the onset of obesity as a result of divorce-related stress (also, the result of too many fast-food meals replacing family dinners at home). I saw depression and poor school performance as a result of stress or deteriorating structure in the home. And I saw the number of school days missed increasing and a host of somatic complaints (headaches, stomach aches) that brought these children to my office.

However, it is important to remember that some children suffer even more when their parents stay together for the sake of "the kids." Being exposed to parents who continually fight and disrespect each other can be even more harmful and have more lasting consequences than a divorce or separation. These same children often grow up to emulate some of these learned behaviors in their own marriages.

I found that many parents, after divorce, could not agree to the same set of household rules as their children went between living quarters. I guess if they could have agreed to something this involved, perhaps they would have had the communication skills in their marriage to avoid divorce in the first place. Remember, kids are resilient. In my experience, they can learn to move back and forth between homes with different rules if those rules are consistently communicated and applied.

Finally, I saw a lot of really bad adult behavior where parents chose the pediatrician's office to play out their unresolved conflicts. For example, they would fail to communicate with each other about scheduled office visits, resulting in double the effort to simply keep everyone informed. More troubling, they would often take opposing sides in complying, or refusing to comply, with suggested medical tests and treatments. Nor was it unusual to see former spouses openly disparage each other in front of their children.

Can divorce or separation be done well? Only with a lot of work and an understanding that the children's best interests come first. What does that look like?

1. Never "fight" in front of your kids, especially at times of planned hand-offs.
2. Meet all your commitments when a schedule is agreed upon and be flexible, if possible, when changes need to be made. See the app Our Family Wizard for a digital assistant to make this happen more easily.
3. Attend doctor visits and school conferences together and be respectful of each other.
4. Make sure to validate the concept that both parents love the child and the child is free to love the other parent.
5. Give children an outlet to express their emotions safely—such as with a counselor. Parents (divorced or not) are rarely ideal best friends.
6. Get professional help yourself if you have a significant mental health or substance abuse problem.

There are many age-appropriate books for children of divorce to read. *Was It the Chocolate Pudding?* for 4-6 years of age and *Divorced but Still My Parents* for 6-12 years of age are two good choices.

Parents might wish to check out the documentary film *SPLIT* (splitfilm. org), possibly viewing it themselves before watching it with their children. This film may validate many of a child's feelings as it follows twelve children speaking about their own experiences in a divorced household.

Pet peeves, or what was most challenging during this period of development

Infants and toddlers rarely are overweight. They eat when they want to and what they need to. And as long as they are provided healthy choices, they remain at a healthy weight. It was only very rarely in my practice that I saw an extremely overweight infant or toddler, and where I suspected a medical condition, I usually referred them to a pediatric endocrinologist. On other rare occasions, an overweight toddler seemed to be the result of rewarding good behavior with "junk food."

Earlier we discussed growth curves. These are part of the vital signs of pediatric practice. It is around the early-school-age years that some children begin the journey toward becoming obese. Unfortunately, this is often a lifetime trip, and research bears this out: fully 50% of obese five- and six-year-olds will remain obese adults (those numbers rise to 90-95% in obese adolescents).

Why does weight gain start at this age? One reason is that children begin to eat away from the home, where choices are not always the best. This can occur at a friend's home, in fast-food restaurants, and even at school. Also, children start to eat for emotional reasons, just as adults do—schoolwork, home life, and not having (or even having) social success can all be stressful.

Sedentary activity plays a role, too, but it is hard to exercise enough to make up for excessive intake. Remember, it is a simple math problem:

Calories in (food) minus calories out (exercise) = net calories per day.

Though recent science about food, intestinal bacteria, and individual differences in metabolism can make this simple equation seem an oversimplification, overeating and taking in excessive calories with unhealthy food and drink choices is a way of life for many households and may foretell weight-gain problems down the road.

What is the pet peeve, or why was weight gain such a difficult problem in my practice? Talk to any pediatrician about their success, or lack thereof, in getting the attention of parents about their child's unhealthy weight. Ask how often parents actually make any, even incremental, changes in their homes (a better place to start than making big changes outside the home) even if they agreed to a plan through tried-and-true techniques such as motivational interviewing, which I often employed. The answers will depress you.

What is motivational interviewing? It is a counseling approach where the patient chooses the changes necessary to be successful after exploring various possible barriers to motivation and the patient's own ambivalence to change. Motivational counseling is different from, and more time consuming than, traditional counseling offered by many physicians in which you are simply told what to do. (For more about motivational interviewing, read *Motivational Interviewing* by William R. Miller and Stephen Rollnick).

Again, like most pet peeves in this book, it is not all on my patients. Perhaps I was a lousy motivational interviewer, though I did study how to do it properly. Yet many of my patients remained an unhealthy weight starting at early school age into their adult lives. Some of the questions I had, and have, include:

- How can we get families to eat together at home, with healthy servings of fruits and vegetables?
- How can we get society to stop marketing high-calorie fast food options to our children?
- What can we do to make healthy foods more affordable and how can we teach food preparation to those who do not have those skills?
- How can we get televisions and computers out of the bedroom and substitute physical activity for sedentary media time?
- How can we motivate or incentivize families and the healthcare system to attend successful programs for weight control that involve frequent follow-up visits to dieticians, psychologists, and other medical personnel?

Kids at this age do not have much money and do not drive cars—who buys them all this stuff to eat, anyway? If it's too easy to say the parents are the whole problem, it's certain they are the biggest part of the solution. When I saw success, it was the result of a commitment on the part of the entire family to make and sustain changes.

Finally: studies suggest parents who exercise, especially mothers, are less likely to have obese children. So, get moving!

Chapter 5

MIDDLE-SCHOOL-AGE CHILDREN

It is a beautiful fall Saturday morning. Both of our kids have soccer games at the same time on opposite sides of the city. Like much of life at this age, it is divide and conquer. Will their teams win? Might one of them even score a goal?

Making friends

Your pediatrician at well-child visits will often ask open-ended questions. I liked to ask the child, how are you doing socially at school? Are you making friends? I was always happy when a child had one or two good friends. Not every child will find the give and take of making friends easy. Learning to navigate the playing field at this age often sets the stage for what will happen during the adolescent and adult years.

Some children are clearly at more risk in this area than others. Autism has socialization issues at the core of its diagnosis as these children misread social cues. Work at developing social skills for these children should start as soon as the diagnosis is made.

Shyness is another diagnosis that can put children at risk when trying to make friends. There is evidence pointing to a genetic basis for being shy. Usually shyness is mild and can be ignored. In any case, it is not a term to use when talking to others about your child and certainly not in front of your child. When severe, it is often associated with anxiety and might better be called social-anxiety disorder. I once heard from a mother about her young son who was mute when in public settings, an extreme form of shyness and anxiety. Social-skills groups at school provided some relief as did medication for anxiety.

By the middle-school years, children are increasingly submerged in the world of their peers. Being accepted, or not, can define children, both to themselves and to others. Socially ostracized children will sometimes hide their exclusion from their parents, and may even refuse to go to school, faking illness in order to stay home.

I was often asked by parents if their children could be "coached up" to deal with their shyness. My answer was yes and no. One problem I saw over the years was parents who did not accept that their child's needs and social skills could be different from their own needs and social success when they were children. Perhaps you were only happiest as the center of attention among your friends— the class president or lead in the school play. Some children are by their nature more comfortable in more intimate settings or while in the background. Accepting your child for who they are is always the best place to start.

But there are times when coaching and teaching social skills might work, especially if the child wants to feel different in specific social situations. For example, role playing can be an effective technique for parents to bolster their child's social skills. Say you are planning a birthday party where the child will need to greet friends and thank them for gifts. Role playing in advance and reviewing how everything went afterward may result in the child's feeling more confident in their social skills. However, be careful not do all the child's "social work" for them and make sure they do not feel judged by you as deficient in some manner if they fail to measure up to your standards.

Assisting a child to identify "friends" who might be "more available" and helping to plan a structured activity can also be tried. This could involve your child's taking a friend to a movie or sporting event that requires a reduced amount of effort to socialize with the other child. It is often better to start with planned activities that are brief, thus increasing the likelihood of the playdate's being successful, rather than planning a long activity such as a sleepover.

When choosing social activities, try to pick one that plays to your child's strengths. Sports may be one of their favorite pastimes, as it is for many children, but some kids might have more social opportunity if their competence is on display in a chess club, a science class, martial arts, or dance. Being attuned to your child's strengths and interests is key in making these choices. And stay out of the way if possible---it is the child who is participating, not the parents. This is the best situation if you are trying to foster independence.

Finally, summer camp, when affordable, can be a huge opportunity to have social success away from home and school. I frequently told parents how strongly I felt about the value of attending summer (that is, sleepover) camps. I believe this opportunity had more to do with my becoming the person I am than any other experience in my life (five years at the same camp for two months each summer from age 10-15). At camp, I was able to test myself and start to see the person that I, not necessarily my parents, wanted to become. Spending time away from home can give children a fresh start and allow them to test their social skills, independence, and self-reliance out from under a parent's watchful eye. It is important to look for a camp that offers activities that match up with your child's interests and has a "camp philosophy" that stresses social-skills growth and respect for all its campers. Sending a child to an away camp is not only good for the child, it can be a learning experience for parents as well. Letting go, as when a child goes off to college or when they get a job and move out of the home for good, can be difficult for some parents. There is no better time to start learning than the present. Isn't that what we tell our kids?

Bullying

When preparing to write this book, I made a list of the topics that I thought parents might want to discuss with their pediatrician. I thought I could tell a story or two from my experience as a physician or my own life that would help make the subjects resonate more. I certainly wanted to write about many of the psychosocial issues one might read about in the daily paper or see on the nightly newscasts.

Bullying seemed a natural topic, but even with over 35 years of practice, I struggle to be able to recount a single story about overt bullying. Perhaps that in and of itself is the most telling reality: All too often, bullying goes undetected and unreported. Bullying might be an underlying cause of a child with school avoidance or depression. Though I am discussing this topic under middle childhood, bullying can take place throughout life and take the form of threats of physical violence, name calling, and cyber bullying. Sometimes an insensitivity about cultural differences (race or religion for example) or how to interact with children with special needs can be problematic for young children. Sometimes, things said, perhaps innocently, are quite hurtful. Regardless of the reasons behind the bullying, it must be identified as it is preventable.

The concept of "mean girls" seems to be in vogue lately. Though I hesitate to speak in stereotypes, boys often just fight and get over slights quickly, whereas girls sometime play out their issues with each other in dramatic fashion. These 'dramas' can become even worse when parents enter the fray, take ownership of the conflicts, and interfere with the opportunity for their daughters to manage these conflicts and learn something.

Many elementary schools have social-skills development and citizenship as part of their learning curriculum. In these programs, kids are learning not only to use their words when confronting a bully but to use body language as well—standing up straight and looking the bully in the eye when voicing their displeasure. Role playing at home may make this challenge easier. Kids at this age are also being taught to speak to a trusted adult if bullying continues. If your school does not have this type of program in place, advocate to start one.

If your child is the bully, get them some help. Perhaps they were bullied themselves somewhere along the way or are struggling with issues of self-esteem. Do not expect it to be a phase they will grow out of without the underlying issues being addressed.

And remember I started this section unable to recount a particular example from my office experience. Because it is difficult to diagnose, parents must be engaged with their kids so that they do not miss clues that bullying is taking place. Talk and LISTEN to your kids. An excellent book to read would be *How To Talk So Kids Will Listen & Listen So Kids Will Talk* by Faber and Mazlish.

Do your Kids have chores?

Raising children to become capable adults has always been challenging. I wonder at times about the loss of traditional expectations in the home, such as doing chores. I know my daughter was perfectly willing to take out the trash, especially as the alternative, clearing the dinner table, was much less desirable to her, while my son never seemed to find doing the dishes too terribly distasteful.

Kids these days are active with school, sports, scouts, dance, music, jobs (teens who want or need to make money), and a multitude of other activities. Parents sometimes use these time commitments to excuse their children from doing jobs around the house. As adults, we, too, are busy and at times it may seem easier for us to complete the chores ourselves instead of badgering our children into doing them.

I suppose for many this may get back to the way you were raised and what values you wish to impart at home. At our home, my wife and I wanted to impart the values of teamwork and responsibility.

To make things easier in assigning chores:

1. Be specific about what is to be done and how often the chores should be completed (a chart might help).
2. Consider letting siblings alternate doing the least desirable chores.
3. Do not expect younger children to do their chores perfectly.
4. Tying an allowance to chores is not necessary, in my opinion, as allowances are part of teaching children how to handle money. Doing chores teaches responsibility and the value of contributing to the home and should not be linked to monetary rewards. Perhaps work around the house outside of the child's normal routine of chores can have financial rewards.

As for appropriate ages for chores and children:

1. Children 3-5 years of age may pick up toys, feed a pet, and put dirty clothes in a basket.

2. Children 5-10 years of age may do the above plus water plants, make their bed, set the table, put the laundry away, and help in the kitchen to prepare simple foods.

3. Children 10 and up can do all of the above plus keep their rooms clean, take out the trash, and unload the dishwasher.

4. Older teens can babysit, mow the grass (after age 12), and help with larger cleaning projects around the house.

So much is changing in our world. Sometimes getting back to basics gets lost in the frenetic pace of our busy lives. Also, today's children are sometimes so enabled by their parents that they develop a sense of entitlement. If your household does not have assigned chores today, get started tomorrow. Someday, your kids will thank you.

Successful children

There are times even in our busy lives that we, parents, have an "Aha! moment." As a pediatrician, I had such a moment one day during a prenatal interview when a young couple asked me how they would know if their child had "turned out O.K." Trying not to impose my values, I asked them what that would look like. They responded by saying they hoped their child would be a productive adult—caring, responsible, available emotionally to experience intimate social relationships. I must confess I held the same aspirations for my own children, although this was not something I shared with the couple at the time.

As a pediatrician, I was not aware of any tools that could monitor a child's progress toward this definition of success. I went looking and found the Search Institute and its age-specific lists of 40 "developmental assets" (search-institute.org/what-we-study/developmental-assets://search-institute.org/what-we-study/developmental-assets) and tools to monitor progress toward acquiring these assets.

Internal Assets

Commitment to Learning

21. **Achievement Motivation**—Child is motivated and strives to do well in school.
22. **Learning Engagement**—Child is responsive, attentive, and actively engaged in learning at school and enjoys participating in learning activities outside of school.
23. **Homework**—Child usually hands in homework on time.
24. **Bonding to school**—Child cares about teachers and other adults at school.
25. **Reading for Pleasure**—Child enjoys and engages in reading for fun most days of the week.

Positive Values

26. **Caring**—Parent(s) tell the child it is important to help other people.
27. **Equality and social justice**—Parent(s) tell the child it is important to speak up for equal rights for all people.
28. **Integrity**—Parent(s) tell the child it is important to stand up for one's beliefs.
29. **Honesty**—Parent(s) tell the child it is important to tell the truth.
30. **Responsibility**—Parent(s) tell the child it is important to accept personal responsibility for behavior.
31. **Healthy Lifestyle**—Parent(s) tell the child it is important to have good health habits and an understanding of healthy sexuality.

Social Competencies

32. **Planning and decision making**—Child thinks about decisions and is usually happy with results of her or his decisions.
33. **Interpersonal Competence**—Child cares about and is affected by other people's feelings, enjoys making friends, and, when frustrated or angry, tries to calm her- or himself.
34. **Cultural Competence**—Child knows and is comfortable with people of different racial, ethnic, and cultural backgrounds and with her or his own cultural identity.
35. **Resistance skills**—Child can stay away from people who are likely to get her or him in trouble and is able to say no to doing wrong or dangerous things.
36. **Peaceful conflict resolution**—Child seeks to resolve conflict nonviolently.

Positive Identity

37. **Personal power**—Child feels he or she has some influence over things that happen in her or his life.
38. **Self-esteem**—Child likes and is proud to be the person that he or she is.
39. **Sense of purpose**—Child sometimes thinks about what life means and whether there is a purpose for her or his life.
40. **Positive view of personal future**—Child is optimistic about her or his personal future.

Search INSTITUTE ❭ 40 Developmental Assets® for Middle Childhood (ages 8-12)

Search Institute® has identified the following building blocks of healthy development—known as Developmental Assets®—that help young people grow up healthy, caring, and responsible.

External Assets

Support

1. **Family support**—Family life provides high levels of love and support.
2. **Positive family communication**—Parent(s) and child communicate positively. Child feels comfortable seeking advice and counsel from parent(s).
3. **Other adult relationships**—Child receives support from adults other than her or his parent(s).
4. **Caring neighborhood**—Child experiences caring neighbors.
5. **Caring school climate**—Relationships with teachers and peers provide a caring, encouraging environment.
6. **Parent involvement in schooling**—Parent(s) are actively involved in helping the child succeed in school.

Empowerment

7. **Community values youth**—Child feels valued and appreciated by adults in the community.
8. **Children as resources**—Child is included in decisions at home and in the community.
9. **Service to others**—Child has opportunities to help others in the community.
10. **Safety**—Child feels safe at home, at school, and in his or her neighborhood.

Boundaries & Expectations

11. **Family boundaries**—Family has clear and consistent rules and consequences and monitors the child's whereabouts.
12. **School Boundaries**—School provides clear rules and consequences.
13. **Neighborhood boundaries**—Neighbors take responsibility for monitoring the child's behavior.
14. **Adult role models**—Parent(s) and other adults in the child's family, as well as nonfamily adults, model positive, responsible behavior.
15. **Positive peer influence**—Child's closest friends model positive, responsible behavior.
16. **High expectations**—Parent(s) and teachers expect the child to do her or his best at school and in other activities.

Constructive Use of Time

17. **Creative activities**—Child participates in music, art, drama, or creative writing two or more times per week.
18. **Child programs**—Child participates two or more times per week in cocurricular school activities or structured community programs for children..
19. **Religious community**—Child attends religious programs or services one or more times per week.
20. **Time at home**—Child spends some time most days both in high-quality interaction with parents and doing things at home other than watching TV or playing video games.

The list of 40 Developmental Assets® is used with permission from Search Institute®. Copyright © 1997, 2006 Search Institute, Minneapolis, MN 55413; www.search-institute.org.

These can be fostered intentionally. They include the "external" assets of support, empowerment, boundaries and expectations, and constructive use of time. "Internal" assets include a commitment to learning, positive values, social competencies, and positive identity. It would be exceedingly rare for any one child to have most of these assets in place. But having more total assets in place, and not being completely wanting in entire category, such as social competence (internal asset) or support (external asset) for example, does predict success in school and in life. Moreover, having fewer assets has been shown to be predictive of an increase in high-risk behaviors such as substance abuse, earlier age of sexual activity, and violent behavior.

Consider exploring the Search Institute site to see where your kids stack up and then make plans to address any gaps. Also consider sharing the site with your school, although they may know about it already or use similar programs for fostering the development of these assets in their students.

There is one category in external assets that is of special significance, in my view. It is service to others: "Child has the opportunity to help others in the community." I feel very strongly that as children this age move into the adolescent years they benefit when doing something outside of themselves. Helping others and similar "services" can help create a healthy perspective to balance the "normal" selfishness of adolescence. This is not to suggest that families wait until middle childhood to introduce this concept. Some families of toddlers might wish to donate their used books and toys to less-privileged children for example. Others might choose to take gifts on Christmas morning to children in the hospital. There are literally countless ways to instill a sense of "doing good" in your children. It's never too early to start making sure they "turn out O.K."

Managing technology and social media

I am writing about this issue under middle childhood because this is the time to act, if you have not already done so. This is not to suggest that you wait to consider the effects of social media and technology on younger children as well. But that should be easier. Most of the use of social media and technology at those ages is under the direct control of parents. If your household is not using these services appropriately at those ages, it might reflect your own use of cell phones, television, and the internet. Or your resorting to the use of these technologies to babysit your child at times.

The American Academy of Pediatrics recommends completely avoiding the use of screen media for children under the age of 18 months, the exception being video chatting. From 18 months to age five, the recommendations are to limit screen media to no more than one hour a day of high-quality programming and to watch with the child to assist them in understanding what they are watching and how it relates to the world around them. Over the age of six, the recommendations are for parents to place consistent limits on time spent using media, on the types of media (there is no place for violent video gaming), and on making sure that media use does not interfere with getting adequate sleep and physical activity.

Snapchat, Instagram, Facebook, ASKfm, WhatsApp, Vine, Twitter, Google+, Kik, Tumblr, Pheed. I imagine by the time of publication of this book there will be others added to the list. Do you even know all of these sites? Perhaps, yes; perhaps, no. Or perhaps some of you use many of them on a daily basis yourselves. I know I had a video chat with my eight-month-old grandson last night and it put a smile on my face.

When thinking about middle-school children, we must remember that the riskiest years—adolescence—are just ahead. Making informed, appropriate decisions now can prevent bigger problems later. Here is a sampling of phone calls I received at my office that might illustrate the challenges of managing social media in your home.

- A single mother of a 12-year-old boy called to discuss her discovery that her son was looking at pornography on the web. He'd run up a bill in excess of $1,000.
- A father called about his 14-year-old daughter. Her best friend's mother had read her own daughter's email (snooping or vigilant?) and learned that both girls had written that they had been sexually active recently (maybe true or false?).

- A mother called about her 12-year-old daughter being sad and unpopular. The daughter had recently posted photos of herself from a ski trip and only received two "likes."
- A father called about his son's poor grades. He asked if his son should be restricted from playing video games on school days. The father admits that he enjoys playing them himself.

With every passing year, I find it more difficult to discern where "life" is taking place. Face-to-face social interaction is disappearing and being replaced with contact through the media. We experience social success and failure through social media (with self-esteem at risk), we can be bullied and harassed through social media (far too easy to say things over the internet), we learn of the moment-to-moment thoughts and digressions of the President of the United States (this is being written in the first 100 days of the Trump presidency), we can share our daily lives, we can video chat with family, we can play games, and we can participate in fantasy leagues with friends who no longer live in the same city, and have a myriad of other "experiences," all through social media.

Most of the use of technology and social media by our children occurs when they are out of our sight. Surveys suggest the average amount of time spent in these areas combined is an astonishing 6-9 hours a day. Though we cannot be physically present at all times, we must have parental presence for this use to decrease to any significant degree and to ensure that, when it does occur, it will have more positive than negative impact.

What is parental presence? We talked about it earlier, but I would like to expand on that conversation here. Writing in the journal *Contemporary Pediatrics* in 1999, Dr. Morris Green suggested that parents with, what he termed, "authoritative presence" had the following characteristics:

- Project authority, confidence, and respect for others.
- Foster family esprit de corps.
- Have high self-esteem.
- Project a sense of efficacy (they know what to do and can do it).
- Model exemplary personal behavior.

- Communicate which behaviors are desirable and acceptable and which are not.
- Promote a child's communication with family members, peers, and teachers.
- Have social supports and can ask for and accept help.
- Motivate a child to comply with parents' behavioral expectations.
- Praise a child for good behaviors and achievements.
- Are knowledgeable about child-development principles.
- Are sensitive to a child's feelings and those of their spouse.
- Spend individual time with each child.
- Succeed in making a child feel loved, admired, and unconditionally accepted.
- Promote a child's social skills.
- Help a child manage anger and resolve conflicts constructively.

What a list to aspire to! Imagine you are that parent. How would you use this "presence" to insure your child's technology and social media uses are for their betterment, not detriment? Some possibilities would be to:

1. Develop household rules to help your child set limits on their use of all kinds of devices. When setting these limits, it is important to distinguish the difference between "passive" and "active use". During the latter, learning and creativity are usually at play and parents might also be involved in working directly with the child. Limit the number of television hours and time spent playing with gaming devices. Turn off cell phones at the dinner table, while doing homework, and after going to bed. Know what Apps are on your child's phone and computer and learn how to use Privacy settings and restrictions available to block inappropriate content and consider having them turn the location services off for some apps to protect their own safety. Let's not be naive about these last suggestions as your child undoubtedly has superior computer skills to the average parent and can circumvent these efforts if they choose to do so.

2. Lead by example in your home and talk to your children about how you handle "media" interruptions in your life and while at work. You cannot expect them to be sitting together with friends and not all be staring down at their cell phones instead of talking, if this is what you model in your personal life. And explain that multitasking while working or studying results in errors and additional time to complete the task at hand.

3. Respect that your child's use of social media is not simply a waste of time. It is part of the current way this age group stays in touch. Some kids are really busy, perhaps even over scheduled, and the use of social media allows them to stay connected. Remind them to manage their safety and reputation (some shared information is out there forever) and encourage them to balance the time spent on these relationships over social media with face-to-face contact. What are generally thought of as adult skills, such as managing conflict, resolving problems, and expressing emotions, are unlikely to develop fully with only internet time as a training ground. Though the negative effects of social media are at times sensationalized, I do believe it is one of the greatest contributors to stress and poor mental health among young people. Like most challenges in savvy parenting, consider all the issues and then act intentionally.

4. Remind middle-school-aged children (and adolescents) to think about what they have written before hitting the send button. Tell them that a ten-minute rule is not a bad idea if the communication could be misconstrued, is inappropriate, offensive, or in violation of their school's student conduct policies.

5. Monitor your child's social media profile if they make it available. I would prefer you not read their diary (just the word suggests this is private), but don't be naive. If their information is not private but out there in the social-media world, monitor it. Some parents actually set up their child's cellphone password and social-media accounts themselves to be certain of access to their information. New products continue to become available to monitor web browsing, filter content, and restrict use of devices to specific time periods. If your child knows these are the rules going in, then there

should be no grounds for complaint. Some families take this one step further and write a formal contract to make sure everyone is on the same page.

6. Encourage your child to take time off. When I was this age, I came home from school and had down time. Now, kids are "branding" themselves 24/7, possibly setting themselves up for no escape or safe space from the social rigors of school life. The resultant anxiety, and at times depression, can become real medical problems. Parents and their kids might want to agree to short periods of time "off the grid" to decompress.

7. Help your child feel good about themselves. FOMO (Fear of Missing Out) and not enough likes to posted photos can be a real problem. Some kids in my office used to describe themselves as feeling invisible. Not only are kids branding themselves on social media, but others are often intentionally (in the form of cyberbullying) or unintentionally (by not "liking" them) branding them as well. Parents must teach their children to define themselves, not to be defined by others. However, this can be easier said than done.

8. Have your child introduce their "friends" and contacts on the internet to you. If you have not met the family or child that is occupying a lot of your child's social time, make arrangements to do so.

The importance of annual well-childcare visits at this age

Your pediatrician will ask that your child come in for yearly physical examinations at this age. Over my years in practice, most parents were very amenable to this recommendation while their child was younger as they were concerned about normal growth and development.

By contrast, the middle-childhood years seem "quiet" to parents next to the excitement of a young child or the challenge of adolescence. Even healthcare professionals can take these pre-adolescent years for granted at times.

So why were these visits important to me, and what did I try to accomplish in them? First, there are many health issues that needed to be monitored more closely at this age. One is the onset of puberty, which can be too early, too late, or can arrest (failure to progress) usually for reasons related to an underlying health problem.

One young woman came in for her age-thirteen physical with no advancement in her pubertal changes over the prior year. At twelve, my notes indicated, she had some breast development and a small amount of pubic hair. There were no further changes at 13. Many detailed questions about possible symptoms of illness were answered negatively, but a blood workup ultimately lead me to pursue further testing, and a diagnosis of inflammatory bowel disease (IBD) was eventually made. Her parents and pediatrician grandfather in another city were thankful, and she felt better, grew better, and had her puberty advance normally after treatment was begun.

Most parents are aware that puberty seems to be starting earlier these last several decades. Your pediatrician, annually, should examine your child for signs of puberty. In girls, this will involve examination of their breasts and pubic hair. In boys, we will be checking testicular size and pubic hair as well. Once these areas are examined, both parents and kids are happy to know that it can be more accurately predicted when their growth spurt will occur and perhaps how tall they will be. As pediatricians, we grade this development by Tanner stages (en.wikipedia.org/wiki/Tannerscale). Your pediatrician can show you and your child these pictures depicting what stage your child is in and what physical and hormonal changes can be expected prior to the next annual exam. Additionally, the stages should be able to predict, fairly accurately, when your daughter will begin menstruation. This is a much-anticipated event that does require preparation (emotionally as well as practically, in the form of supplies) and signifies that your child can reproduce. Similarly, the pediatrician can also predict when your son will be capable of reproducing (this may be marked by wet dreams). It is a rare parent who wants to contemplate the reproductive ramifications of advancing puberty at these ages, but sexual maturity can occur as young as 10 in women (the average age is 12 1/2) and 11 in boys (average: 13 1/2). These reproductive ramifications are too important not to acknowledge in any event. If puberty is occurring too early or too late, a pediatric endocrinologist may need to be consulted. This assessment of puberty is part of an ongoing conversation about sex and sexuality your pediatrician will have with you and your middle-school-aged child. Making sure these annual visits occur allows for both the parent and child to see their pediatrician as a resource in these matters before moving forward into adolescence.

Another health issue at this age is monitoring your child's spine for the possible development of scoliosis (curvature of the spine). Fortunately, most children with scoliosis will have mild forms that only require more-frequent examinations during this period of rapid growth and perhaps an X-ray. However, significant scoliosis, requiring bracing and, rarely, surgery, can occur. In my practice, it always seemed the worst cases were in kids I had not seen for a physical exam in quite some time. They may have been in the office for a respiratory illness or a minor injury, but at these visits, their spines may not have been examined.

Other important physical issues that may require attention in this age group include possible treatment for acne, blood pressure, and complications of obesity, just to name a few. As families do not want to be inattentive to any of these issues, it's another reason for the importance of bringing their child in to see their pediatrician on a regular basis so that they may get proper and timely diagnoses and, if needed, treatments.

An even more important benefit of annual checkups than these health issues, in my opinion, is the chance to further the pediatrician's relationship with both the child and the parent. These kids need to know who we are. They need to see their pediatrician as an adult in "their universe" who has information and experience and their best interests at heart. This can only happen when annual visits occur in your pediatrician's office and certainly not in an urgent care center or walk-in clinic.

Before retiring, I frequently taught medical-school students and residents. I told them that all my office visits prior to adolescence were focused, on some level, on preparing families (both parent and child) to place their trust in the doctor-patient relationship. Becoming a trusted resource to families during adolescence was what made pediatrics special to me.

Is it best to see a pediatrician of the same sex?

I was asked this question often by parents of children in this age group, and sometimes by the patients themselves. As a male physician, I could not imagine only taking care of male adolescent patients. I imagine my female colleagues over the years would say the same about only seeing young women.

My response, though always to accommodate ultimately whatever the family wanted, was to resist this suggestion. I would simply tell the mother or father that physicians are no more male or female than teachers or policemen are. Coming to the office and being examined is not a sexual event—although, when parents choose to change to a same sex pediatrician for this reason, it may reaffirm that notion.

There will be discussions at times about puberty and sexuality. One advantage of having an opposite-sex physician is the opportunity to have these discussions comfortably and safely, which can be a model for conversations about intimacy with a partner down the line.

Whenever this issue arose, often in the form of a phone call, I would ask the family to make their next appointment with me and at that time, I would discuss the issue directly with the patient and parents and usually together we would make a decision that left everyone happy. Ultimately, the patient had to be clearly comfortable and make the decision themselves. Using this approach over the years allowed me to take care of adolescents of both sexes. It may or may not come as a surprise, but it was harder to get women to move on from my pediatric practice at age 22 than it was their male counterparts.

Anxiety disorders

Over the years, I received many calls from concerned parents about their children's behaviors. A few of the incidents, and my diagnoses, as retrieved from my patient charts:

- As mentioned earlier, a mother called to ask me how concerned she should be that her son would not talk in social situations (social anxiety and mutism).
- A mother of an eighth-grade student called to ask if I could write a letter explaining why he had not been to school in over two months. During this period of time, there had been a few calls about mild infections but no office visits (school avoidance, social phobia).
- A 13-year-old girl was sent to my office by the school nurse to evaluate an episode in which she complained of not being able to breathe and almost passing out in science class when students were dissecting a frog. The girl also complained of her hands and feet becoming numb and tingly (panic attack isolated to science class).

I have chosen to discuss anxiety disorders during the middle-school-age of development because that age is usually the time it first comes to medical attention. This is not to say that some younger, and some older, children do not meet the criteria as well.

I am not talking here about simply being "anxious." After all, we all feel anxious at times for both real and imagined reasons. Perhaps learning to re-calibrate how we filter what seems a daily onslaught of information and trouble in the world would benefit everyone. Perhaps we need to manage or "unplug" from our cell phones, emails, and televisions. Perhaps multitasking is not something to be proud of.

Anxiety disorders are different. In my practice, they were the most frequent mental-health diagnosis I was called upon to make and treat. There is no doubt that over my 35 years of practice they were on the rise, and in some people's minds, rising to epidemic proportions. In these children, their "anxiety" interfered with daily activities, a necessary component to make the diagnosis. Some kids did not wish to go to school, fly on an airplane, attend birthday parties and sleepovers, or order in a restaurant. It might be that the increase in cases is simply that the diagnosis is being recognized and treated more as a result of both education and pressure from pharmaceutical companies to prescribe their medications. Undoubtedly, the society pressures and media experiences mentioned earlier are also playing a role as the "need" to defend one's social reputation 24/7 has enormous implications as an anxiety accelerator in children and adolescents.

Perhaps the biggest opportunity to help these kids resides in how a parent's responses and behavior with an anxious child can allow them to become more resilient when facing situations that make them uncomfortable. When parents have their children avoid a stressful situation completely or make too many accommodations to shield their children from the anxiety provoking situation, they lose out on learning how to handle them and next time will be the same or even worse. In addition, this type of parental action can reinforce that the fear is actually real. It may be hard to sit back and watch your child struggle a bit, but this is the best path to real learning and building the confidence to face the very situations that cause distress.

Though different from depression (which we will discuss in our adolescent chapter), treatment for anxiety disorders is similar with the use of CBT (cognitive behavioral therapy) and SSRIs (selective serotonin re-uptake inhibitors) being the best options. In my experience, most parents are comfortable with this diagnosis and suggested treatments because often they suffer from the same disorder (a strong family history is common), and, therefore, have insight into the benefits of having a treatment plan in place. In addition, since they themselves have been living with the condition for some time, they have usually moved on from any feelings that the diagnosis carries a social stigma.

In treating anxiety disorders, I always preferred to start with CBT alone and would only add medications if there were persistent problems with daily living. Some parents seemed surprised that I rarely suggested an anti-anxiety medication, particularly considering that this was sometimes how their own condition was being managed. I was very fearful that this type of "as-needed" treatment of taking a Xanax from time to time, would eventually be misused and abused, creating further difficulties. Furthermore, I could not imagine putting a child in the position of thinking they needed a pill for any or all situations. Therefore, I preferred to use a daily SSRI medication for at least 6-12 months, with the expectation that we would wean the child off medication within one year of starting. This is a "best practice" medical recommendation, though contrary to the experience of many parents who had been taking medication for years without an attempt to see how they would do off the medication.

The key to stopping medication successfully was the therapy (CBT). This required a lot of pushing as most families preferred the quick fix of medication to the time required to successfully benefit from CBT.

Anxiety disorders are further classified into generalized anxiety disorder, separation anxiety disorder, social phobia, and panic disorder. Obsessive-compulsive disorder and post-traumatic stress disorder are often grouped separately from the above-mentioned disorders as their treatments may need to be more specific to the underlying cause.

Let your pediatrician know if you have concerns about your child's mental health. And do not be surprised if a mental-health diagnosis needs to be made when your child presents to the office with physical complaints (as we will see in the upcoming chapter on adolescence, where we discuss stress and how it can present in the form of conversion reactions, somatization disorders, and eating disorders).

Pet peeves, or what was most challenging during this period of development

Middle childhood represents a period when matters of physical health, mental health, academic issues, and social life come together. In this chapter, I mentioned that not having annual visits during these years can put families who have medical challenges at a disadvantage, because they will lack the strong doctor-patient relationship needed later to navigate adolescent problems.

However, even families I did see on a regular basis often hid from me that they (that is, their children) were at risk for problems. Perhaps they hid things or perhaps they could not see the risk clearly themselves. Perhaps I did not ask enough, or the right, questions, or did not use enough screening instruments to detect the clouds on the horizon.

But frequently, problems appeared out of the blue. A phone call about academic failure, substance abuse, school refusal (one child had not been to school for over six months), pregnancy, or suicide would send me back to my medical records where I would see that at the last annual exam there had been no problems mentioned.

When my patients were under the care of a surgeon or medical subspecialist, I would always be kept apprised of their progress by means of a detailed report about their diagnosis and treatment. However, when my patients were seeing a mental-health professional, this type of information was not always communicated to me. Even more often, these patients with mental-health issues were not under anyone's care because no formal diagnosis had been made.

At times, it can be difficult for parents to share concerns about family situations. They may feel judged, stigmatized, or shamed. Your physician knows better. The exam room is a safe place. We want to know all of your concerns about your child. We want to know if something in a child's home or immediate environment could cause difficulties. It may take some extra time or an additional visit, but often, if we have all the information, we can help.

Chapter 6

ADOLESCENCE

It is midnight and my son is not home yet despite this being his curfew. It has happened in the past. Usually he calls to tell us he is on his way from somewhere close by. Tonight, he has not called. We try not to be too nervous or angry. When he does walk in a 12:15 we ask him to call next time if he will be late.

Any discussion of children between the ages of 15 and 22 is complicated by the normal physical and psychological differences this age range encompasses. In a perfect world, at the end of adolescence parents are ready to unleash their children onto the world well prepared to become responsible, honest, and compassionate adults capable of emotionally intimate relationships and of contributing in their chosen field of work and in their community. Some may be surprised to see my grouping these young people together until 22 years of age. I have chosen that age because I encouraged most of my patients to stay with me as their physician until completing college. Medical care can become very erratic when adolescents leave home for college, and staying with their pediatrician allows for consistent quarterbacking of medical and emotional issues by someone well known and respected by both the adolescent and their parents.

Keeping in mind the goal—competent, self-reliant, caring adults—here are my thoughts on navigating these years successfully.

Confidentiality

The following statement was crafted by my group practice and distributed to families during their well-child adolescent visits:

> We encourage adolescents to begin assuming responsibility for their health. We may perform part of the interview and examination with the parents out of the room. A chaperone is available upon request. Parents and their teenage children should discuss this matter in advance of their visit so that we may abide by their preferences. It is most helpful if we know of any parental concerns in advance of the appointment. We maintain confidentiality regarding our discussion with adolescent patients. We will inform parents if an adolescent is posing a threat to him/herself or someone else. We encourage parents to maintain open communications with their adolescent.

As I mentioned in the chapter on middle childhood, much of my practice time and effort was spent preparing patients and their families for this next stage in our relationship when information could be shared confidentially. Receiving a phone call from an adolescent or having them ask me a "personal" question while they were in the office was not necessarily something I relished, but it did confirm that the message of confidentially had gotten across. Though many of these questions continued to remain a "secret," I was often able to convince my adolescent patients that sharing them with their parents could be beneficial. Ultimately, this was their choice unless, as mentioned in the confidentiality statement, there was the possibility of imminent harm to themselves or others. This privilege to be a "most-trusted adult" in the lives of my patients was probably the single most gratifying part of my pediatric practice career.

Confidentiality is not to be confused with consent to treatment and the concept of emancipated minors. State and national laws govern consent issues. For example, some parents are surprised to learn how the law regards treatment of sexually transmitted infections and substance abuse, or obtaining birth control. It's important that you make yourself familiar with your state's laws or ask your pediatrician in advance about how these issues will be handled.

Trust

In our chapter on infants, the concept of trust during the adolescence years was mentioned in discussing the role of grandparents and their efforts to garner the trust of the very children they raised so that they might play a role in the life of their grandchildren.

Trust is at the center of the adolescent years. When adolescents bend, break, or ignore household rules, something has to give. Usually there are repercussions and, at times, punishment. It is always best if the adolescent knows what the consequences will be in advance. This avoids parents' making it all up on the fly. "Grounding" seems to be the go-to choice of most parents.

But does grounding really work? Some kids care little when things are taken away. Some will say they have nothing left to lose, so the behavior continues. Studies suggest that adolescents, in contrast to adults, are more motivated to seek rewards than to avoid punishment. It reminds me of the time my son inadvertently asked two different girls to a school dance and got grounded intentionally in order to avoid having to explain his mistake to the girls. (Of course, he asked us for permission to go to the after-dance parties—did he think we were idiots?) If you are truly trying to motivate an adolescent to make better decisions, consider rewarding them with car privileges, a few dollars, or lifting a grounding period a day or two early.

If you do use grounding, make sure you do not strip your child of every choice and every freedom. Try to avoid taking away non-academic activities where they excel (e.g., sports, theatre, chess) as this is where they get their self-esteem, do not cut them off from all social contact (for example, cannot go out but may use social media to some degree), and make the restrictions for a reasonable length of time (no more than one week). The sooner the child can resume their pre-grounding routine and face the same difficult decisions, the sooner they can demonstrate that a lesson was learned. When denied the opportunity to correct, or learn from, the ill-advised behavior, the adolescent has no means to regain your trust. Navigating the relationship with an adolescent can be difficult enough without your making it harder by policing your child. When raising my two children, though it was never easy to fall asleep before their curfew (midnight, stretching to 1 A.M. after they were 18), eventually I was able to do so after they demonstrated their maturity to make good, safe decisions. This did not occur right away, but it was well worth the wait (and anxiousness).

Some adolescent mistakes involve more than breaking household rules. Some are truly misdeeds, like stealing or vandalism, where someone or something was harmed. Logical consequences and reparation are more appropriate in these circumstances. Apologizing to the injured party and coming to an agreement on working the transgression off are best practices when such situations occur. If a law has been broken and the legal system is involved, there is a temptation to use whatever influence you might have to "get them off." I can recall several situations when this seemed on some level to condone poor behavior and may have contributed to additional mistakes and legal problems.

There is often an unrecognized conflict when parenting decisions for adolescent children involve safety versus control. It can be hard at times to tease out the difference. Perhaps two examples might help. Suppose your child wants your permission to go to a theme park with friends for the evening without any adult supervision. You could say no (meeting our own need to not have to deal with the worry of a possibly unsafe outcome), or you could allow the adolescent to go but say that you intend to go on your own that night as well (separately) to see for yourself that they will be safe. Then, the next time they ask to go, you can make a decision truly based on safety. Or say it is time for college and you want your child to sign up for a preparation course for the SAT or ACT admissions test to help them get into the "best college" possible. Your child does not want to take the course. You could have a conversation stressing why you think taking the course is a good idea and then let your child decide, but instead you offer them $500 to take the course asserting your control over the ultimate decision.

Safety is a real concern and a place where parents should assert their authority. In our first example, the theme park might be unsafe—you have every right to see for yourself. You might find that your anxiety is mostly unwarranted, and it will be an excellent opportunity for your adolescent to make their own "safe" decisions and grow in the process. In the second example, the parent is trying to motivate with a reward, pushing the child, the parent hopes, to make a good decision. The problem is that the push is coming from the outside—that is, from you. The adolescent's opportunity to define themselves and whom they want to be is being taken away by the parent's assertion of control. Is this a path toward building self-esteem and self-reliance for the child? Watch out for all decisions where control and your own anxiety are the major forces at work. Such "boundary" issues and decisions may be at odds with that which most parents are trying to achieve at his age for their children.

As I've said, trust is at the core of the adolescent-parent relationship. There were countless times in my office where the issue of trust came up. The teen breaks the rules and the parent responds by threats, invasions of privacy, and guilt trips. The relationship is breaking down and needs to be reset. How can this be accomplished in a way that helps your child? Here a few possibilities.

1. Stop talking *at* each other, screaming and threatening, and start communicating. Try to decide *with your child* what trust will look like in your home. What should you expect of each other? As a parent, you do not wish to be your child's best friend. The job of a parent is to fairly, lovingly, and consistently set limits and to be respectful when doing so. As an adolescent, their "job" is to push boundaries and become more independent. Negotiate the rules together and get to a better place, even as you recognize and acknowledge the difference between safety and control. There should be more give than take on your part if the latter is primarily at work.

2. Motivate with rewards, not punishment. When expectations are being met, give your child praise and new privileges when deserved. This is different than the $500 "bribe" to take the SAT preparatory class we discussed a few pages ago where it was more about "control".

3. As a parent, be prepared for bumps in the road. When the next "mistake" occurs, do not compound it by going back to your old

behaviors of being a frustrated parent, and further breaking down whatever trust you have built. Count to ten or maybe wait until the next morning before reacting. Ideally, you and your adolescent should both be finding your way together toward a more mature and mutually rewarding relationship.

4. When mistakes are made, do not compound the situation by "enabling" the bad behavior. When an adult steps-in to make the situation "right" or takes on the responsibility or blame themselves, it robs the adolescent of a learning experience and may shield them from the real need to change their behavior and make more responsible choices in the future.

5. Find an interest to share or make time for a one-on-one breakfast to learn about one of your adolescent's interests that you do not share. After all, your children are going to leave soon enough and you will no longer have these opportunities. Seeing each other as people (though not best friends) is realistic and rewarding.

6. Even when there is conflict, make sure your child knows that they are loved unconditionally.

7. Eat dinner as a family as often as possible, if not nightly. I hope this has been part of your family routine all along. Whether the resulting discussions are far reaching or trivial, I am certain the time spent together will contribute greatly to an improved relationship with your child.

Sex, drugs, and rock 'n' roll

I suppose just this title shows my age. I did not attend Woodstock (1969) but wish I had. Adolescence is as much about making choices as it is about anything else. The part of the brain that is linked to thinking before acting is called the prefrontal cortex, an area of the brain that continues to grow into one's adult years. Thinking before we act is also a matter of experience and risk avoidance and is learned over time as well. The hope for young people, and their parents, is that the mistakes are not too big. I would often say to parents that if adolescents are meant to learn from their mistakes, my kids would probably be geniuses by now.

Sex and intimacy

- A fourteen-year-old girl had a snow day (school canceled) and spent it at home alone with her boyfriend. They had sex and the condom broke. At last year's checkup, when informed by the girl that she had begun to menstruate, she and I discussed (her mother was present) abstinence and forms of birth control including emergency contraception. After the incident with her boyfriend, she called my office for emergency contraception, which by law must be prescribed without parental consent or knowledge.
- A sixteen-year-old girl called my home (phone number unlisted) on a Saturday afternoon because she was contemplating having sex that night with her boyfriend. Together, we decided it was a bad idea, and it did not happen.
- A college junior called about being depressed. He had not discussed the issue with his steady girlfriend of six months despite the closeness of their relationship. They were sexually active and using birth control. When I advised him that this intimate relationship could involve sharing with her his concern about being depressed and that I thought it might be helpful, he chose to do so. Her subsequent support played a large role in his dealing successfully with his depression.
- A male college student inquired at the end of his routine physical if he could ask me a personal question. His orgasms when masturbating were not as powerful as when he was having sex with his girlfriend. We had a long conversation about sex and intimacy.
- When asked if she was sexually active, an adolescent female told me yes. When I inquired about what form of contraception she was using, she told me she did not need any. Her "boyfriend" was biologically a girl. When I asked if she had ever been sexually active in the past, she said yes but that that "boyfriend" had also been

99

a girl. When I asked her if she was attracted sexually to males (heterosexual) or females (gay/homosexual), she indicated males.

- When discussing a young man's sexual development, I mentioned he might experience a wet dream. His mother had never heard of that and seemed incredulous that they actually occurred. Two years later, her daughter had an unwanted pregnancy. Some families are unable to provide sexual education to their children without help and support from their physician or other trusted resources. Leaving this responsibility to a school health teacher can rob parents of their opportunity to share not just information about sex but their values.

I could go on and on, but you probably get the picture. Perhaps you have noticed in the book that I intentionally brought up sexuality issues with parents starting with their child's infancy. An individual who was a big influence on me professionally, Jocelyn Elders, the U.S. surgeon general from 1993-1994, made it clear how important it was for the doctor's office to be a place to talk safely about sexuality, a position with which I completely agreed, and one I put into practice. The effort on my part to talk (and listen) openly and honestly about sexuality, encouraged by Elders' example, was often mentioned by patients and parents in their feeling comfortable and asking me questions.

Adolescence is marked by many important events including the physical changes of puberty culminating in the ability to reproduce and an interest in genital sexual behaviors. When I first started practice, in 1981, I spent most of my efforts counseling patients to delay sexual activity due to the risk of pregnancy and sexually transmitted infections. (I was never particularly impressed that my counsel was working very well.) I provided birth-control information with a strong emphasis on abstinence, but also made sure that all patients who had physically matured to the point where they could have a baby received information on other methods of birth control including condoms, oral contraceptives, long-acting reversible contraception including injections, IUDs and sub-dermal implants, and emergency contraception.

One would think that the use of condoms with every sexual encounter is a given these days with the knowledge of sexually transmitted infections (STIs), but unfortunately that is not the case among those in committed relationships as well as those in more casual ones. A simple question I sometimes asked adolescents in the office went like this: "How many times do you have to have sex to catch a sexually transmitted infection?" Obviously, the answer is one. My message in the office was simple and straightforward: it is disrespectful to yourself and your partner not to use protection. Since many STIs are asymptomatic, one cannot count on a partner's not having an infection short of recent testing. Serious complications of STIs include infertility, tubal pregnancies, reproductive-system cancers, transmission of infection to a fetus, pelvic inflammatory disease (PID), epididymitis, genital pain, and HIV. While in practice I promoted this simple rule: if there are no condoms available on the night in question, there can be no sex.

My advice about birth control choices did not change over the years, but I did develop new ways to talk about why abstinence was my preferred option. With the adolescent's parents present, I would ask my patients what were two "good" reasons for anyone, at any age, to have sex. Most would correctly answer to have a baby and agree that they were not interested in that at this time. Many would be stumped about the second reason, but most commonly they said if they were in love. Actually, I was looking for pleasure (orgasm) as the answer, though love plays a role in that as well. One does not need to have an orgasm every time for sex to be good between two consenting adults. But in my experience, adolescent females almost never have orgasms with their partners despite "being in love." The adolescent female and I would then have a discussion about sex—that it requires both physical and emotional intimacy to be rewarding. I challenged them to consider if "enough" was really going on emotionally in these relationships to justify having sex. Similarly, I would ask the boys in my office if they would like to have sex when the outcome was a possible pregnancy and no orgasm for themselves. I did not get a lot of takers. I challenged these boys to ask their girlfriends if they were experiencing orgasms when they had sex. If the answer was no, I asked these boys to discuss whether their partner was still comfortable having sex and suggested stopping if not. We would then have a conversation about physical and emotional intimacy similar to the one I had with my female patients.

Often with patients I used an analogy comparing sex to tennis. You can play a set or two of tennis with a random partner and not get a lot of exercise. But if you play with a perfectly matched partner, it is a better game. Adolescents who choose to become sexually active are not getting much exercise, if you will. In fact, I really cannot think of too many teens in my experience who were emotionally capable of the type of intimacy I believe is needed to make the decision to have sex become part of real emotional growth. I tell these adolescents that sex has to be more than putting your body parts together. You need to put *yourselves* together. However, let's make sure no one thinks this discussion is unnecessary as studies show that nearly 50% of teens are sexually active before leaving high school. I just want to do something about it.

The last part of the conversation I had in my office about sex involved asking a parent, in front of their teen, if they wanted their child to become sexually active someday. This question surprised both parent and child. But it gave parents an opportunity to articulate something that most would like to say but do not know how or in what context to say it. And of course, the answer was yes. The parents would often add words to the effect that only when both partners were mature enough so that it is more than just a physical act. You should be physically and emotionally ready, they would say, it should be with someone you trust, and it must be your choice. What parent would not say that? Some parents would add other qualifiers, such as "when you are married," to which I would not disagree. It represented their values and was good to state clearly. As important as these conversations in the office were, I know that the most important conversations on sex and sexuality are the ones that occur at home between parent and child. Have them. If you do not, your kid's information will come from their friends, other adults, media, and the internet (even pornographic websites which is truly regrettable). The information may or may not be accurate and, as stated before, will not necessarily reflect your values.

I think there have always been a couple of less obvious reasons for much of the sexual activity we see today. The first is about self-esteem and girls seeking approval from their peers (both male and, maybe more important, female) by being sexually active. The second is that adult role models speak up about all kinds of things, but not sex. Women and men need to hear from their parents and especially from trusted and respected adults in their life. One of my frustrations over the years involved mother & daughter teas for sexual education and father & son dinners for the same. What topic could my daughter hear about where my presence as a father would not add something. And the same could be said about my wife and my son. Most of my conversations in the office occurred with the adolescent and mother, and mothers would tell me, their husbands would find these conversations too awkward to initiate or participate in. So, I say to you fathers, please have these conversations with your daughters. I say to you mothers, please have these conversations with your sons. I say to all parents, have these conversations with all your children. You will be surprised at their value.

Dating—for and against

Currently, most kids socialize in groups. When I asked parents in the office, "At what age will you allow your child to date?" the most oft-given answer was 30—and this was not said tongue in cheek. Though an absolute age does not take into account issues of emotional maturity, I would usually opt for sixteen or so.

Speaking generally, if it were put to a vote, I would vote for dating. You do not want your son or daughter to marry the first person who smiles back at them. Dating does not have to mean sex, but it can be a time to explore and learn about emotional intimacy with all its give and take. I always wanted my children to learn how to develop meaningful relationships and to recognize exploitative or manipulative ones. This can only occur with practice and when it is modeled in the home.

Many parents fear their adolescent will be a victim of dating violence. This can be physical, sexual, psychological, or emotional. It can take place face to face or over electronic media. It is reasonable to be more reticent if your child has a mental health diagnosis like depression or anxiety which can predispose them to thinking that these abusive relationships are acceptable. However, like many parental fears, our children cannot learn unless given an opportunity to try.

Some cultures and religions do not permit dating and limit contact between the sexes at this age. When parents insist on an adolescent's following these rules, there can be conflict. Helping parents deal with this conflict usually proved difficult for me. While to the adolescent, it seemed more about control than anything else, to the adult, it could be the very core of their religious faith and values. When all parties are respectful of one another, generally children accept most of their parent's values over time if not necessarily during the adolescent years themselves.

Substance use and abuse

Identifying adolescents who are using drugs can be difficult. Though over the years in my office some adolescents freely admitted in front of their parents to frequent marijuana use (claiming it was not affecting them adversely nor were they going to stop), most chose to hide their use. Many parents seemed to condone alcohol use accepting it as a normative adolescent behavior.

To frame our discussion, perhaps a few examples of phone calls I received might be helpful.

- The father of 17-year-old male called to ask if I would secretly test his son for drugs. When asked why he suspected his son was using drugs, he replied that he smelled it on his clothes and that his grades were dropping. When I asked him what "we" would need to do if he tested positive, he said he was not sure. And when I asked him if he had asked his son about drug use, he responded that he had not.
- A mother called to inform me that her 16-year-old son had died the night before of a heroin overdose. She had not been aware of his drug use. At his last physical examination, no problems had been uncovered.
- A mother called about her 18-year-old son's minor auto accident. He'd been drinking but no charges were pressed and the officer simply brought him home. Upon further questioning, she admitted concern that drinking may be a problem for the son, but she was not ready for him to receive medical "treatment" yet. The divorced father's opinion was similar. The following year at college it became clear to all that ignoring the problem was not helping anyone as

additional incidents occurred. Ultimately, the son became abstinent through AA.

What are the substances in play among young people currently? In alphabetical order, they are alcohol, club drugs (GHB, ketamine, LSD, Rohypnol), cocaine, hallucinogens, heroin, inhalants, marijuana, MDMA (ecstasy), methamphetamines, opioids, prescription drugs and OTC cold medications, steroids (anabolic), synthetic cannabinoids (K2), synthetic cathinones (bath salts), and tobacco/nicotine. E-cigarettes usually are used with e-liquids containing nicotine but not always. Though over the years I treated patients who had experimented with all of these drugs, alcohol, marijuana, and cigarettes were the most common problems. Though less widespread, heroin is out there and in use, and its risk for causing fatalities is obviously not to be minimized.

Data from the National Institute on Drug Abuse indicate that by the senior year of high school, 70% of students will have tried alcohol, 50% an illicit drug, 40% cigarettes, and 20% a prescription drug for non-medical purposes. Repeated studies support the notion that earlier use is predictive of more-significant problems as adolescents get older.

How can we suspect substance abuse, when is it properly called a disorder, what can we do to treat it, what can we do to prevent it, and what should we say to the father who wishes for me to screen his son for drugs?

First, when should you suspect that your child has a problem? The father in the phone call mentioned smelling marijuana on his son's clothing. Sometimes changes in hygiene and appearance are important clues (during one physical exam I saw needle tracks). Another tipoff can be mood changes— sadness, silence, secrecy. Behavioral issues such as sneaking out, making new friends, auto accidents, and sleeping more are suspicious signs. As are school problems which might include changes in grades or behavior, truancy, or quitting a favorite activity or sports team. Finally, having money or valuables disappearing or finding drug paraphernalia in the home should be very worrisome. Don't be surprised if when confronted the adolescent insists that someone else was responsible for the theft or the paraphernalia. If you suspect your child has a drug problem, be careful about snooping, and if you plan to search their room regularly, tell them you plan to do so because privacy only goes so far when safety is the issue.

A substance-abuse disorder exists when continued use of a drug is associated with impaired control (longer use, being unsuccessful in cutting back, spending excessive time on use), social impairment (affecting schoolwork and relationships with friends and family), risks (injuries, auto accidents), and signs of pharmacologic dependence, tolerance, and withdrawal. The problem in my office was getting adolescents to admit that drug use had become a problem: occupying too much time, hurting school performance and affecting interpersonal relationships. They were often intransigent about their denial. Some even suggested they needed to keep using marijuana because it helped to calm them down and was helping their grades. Even more tragically, sometimes the abuse, especially of alcohol, only comes to light after a fatal auto accident or an episode of sexual violence. I will discuss these two issues later under adolescent safety.

What can be done to treat a drug disorder? First is getting the adolescent to admit there is a problem and to recognize they need help. Because their period of substance abuse is often not very long (as compared to an adult's), it can be difficult to get them to make a serious commitment to treatment since the consequences of their abuse have been fewer or are deemed insignificant by the adolescent themselves. While deteriorating grades may mean a lesser college or no college at all, "big deal" may be their response. Some get to treatment by mandate from juvenile authorities, but relapse is often the norm until more disappointments in life occur. Moreover, many of these kids have an undiagnosed mental health disorder, which must be addressed and treated properly as well.

I am not enamored of in-patient treatment settings unless a patient needs to be detoxified. Thirty-day programs often seem designed more for one size fits all, and their duration conveniently matches the number of days insurance will cover. Real recovery will require a lengthy, ongoing program. Outpatient treatment seems to have better results in my experience. Some families send their children to "boot camps" in remote areas of the country. Though these programs remove patients from some of the social milieu associated with their drug abuse and mental health problems, I cannot recommend them under any circumstances. This is because many of the programs lack accreditation and have been reported to subject residents to physical and psychological abuse. In addition, parents are often asked to sign documents giving these camps temporary custody of their child.

As we have mentioned in prior chapters, prevention is the hallmark of pediatrics. Your pediatrician may routinely use a CRAFFT questionnaire to identify youth at risk for substance abuse. The adolescent completes this confidentially.

The CRAFFT Questionnaire (version 2.0)

Please answer all questions **honestly**; your answers will be kept **confidential**.

During the PAST 12 MONTHS, on how many days did you:

1. Drink more than a few sips of beer, wine, or any drink containing **alcohol**? Put "0" if none.

   ☐ # of days

2. Use any **marijuana** (pot, weed, hash, or in foods) or "**synthetic marijuana**" (like "K2" or "Spice")? Put "0" if none.

   ☐ # of days

3. Use **anything else to get high** (like other illegal drugs, prescription or over-the-counter medications, and things that you sniff or "huff")? Put "0" if none.

   ☐ # of days

READ THESE INSTRUCTIONS BEFORE CONTINUING:
- If you put "0" in ALL of the boxes above, ANSWER QUESTION 4, THEN STOP.
- If you put "1" or higher in ANY of the boxes above, ANSWER QUESTIONS 4-9.

	No	Yes
4. Have you ever ridden in a **CAR** driven by someone (including yourself) who was "high" or had been using alcohol or drugs?	☐	☐
5. Do you ever use alcohol or drugs to **RELAX**, feel better about yourself, or fit in?	☐	☐
6. Do you ever use alcohol or drugs while you are by yourself, or **ALONE**?	☐	☐
7. Do you ever **FORGET** things you did while using alcohol or drugs?	☐	☐
8. Do your **FAMILY** or **FRIENDS** ever tell you that you should cut down on your drinking or drug use?	☐	☐
9. Have you ever gotten into **TROUBLE** while you were using alcohol or drugs?	☐	☐

The first three questions have been carefully worded to encourage adolescents to honestly disclose their frequency of substance use, but also to suggest that non-use is normal. If there has been any use in the prior 12 months, the patient is asked to answer questions #4-9. All patients are asked to answer question #4 about riding in a CAR driven by someone (including themselves) who was high or had been using drugs or alcohol.

Each positive response in questions #4-9 increases the probability that the adolescent has a substance abuse problem and allows us to get started in providing an appropriate level of treatment. This could simply involve counseling in the pediatrician's office. Other times, referral to a mental health professional well versed in substance abuse is more appropriate. As mentioned earlier, thirty-day inpatient programs, in my opinion, offer little for the vast majority of adolescent patients with substance abuse issues.

When the CRAFFT screen was negative, I would usually praise the adolescent for their decision making to date. Though adolescents are not programmed to think about the future, I would often ask them about their goals in the next 2-5 years and remind them that substance use and abuse would likely interfere with achieving those goals (getting into the college of their choice was often an expressed goal).

What additional advice did I find useful for families who wished to prevent a substance abuse problem?

- Sitting together for family meals at the dinner table
- Being an authoritative *adult* parent with clear household rules. (This would not include trying to be the "cool" parent who buys a keg of beer for the kids at their home—this happened in my practice.)
- Talking about the dangers of drug use
- Being involved in community organizations—both parent and adolescent
- Having parents of your teen's closest friends be authoritative as well

Back to the father who wished for me to screen his son's urine without his knowledge. What did I tell him? I informed him that I would not be able to honor his request. First, it would be both unethical and illegal. I did tell him that we could perform the screening with his son's knowledge as long as we, additionally, had a plan in place to discuss the results. My practice's policy on confidentiality allowed me an "out" to breach confidentiality if I believed the patient was at risk for significant harm to himself or others based on the results of testing. A positive marijuana screen, however, would unlikely be divulged to parents without the adolescent's permission; drugs such as heroin would be different. I also suggested to the father that he discuss his concerns directly with his son. Indicating why he was worried about him might open lines of communication and ultimately improve the outcome in any event.

My second reason for declining the father's request was that something as simple and straightforward as a frank and honest talk between a doctor and patient can bring the necessary information into the open. This particular child might admit to me, confidentially, the extent of his substance use. I am not suggesting that kids didn't lie to me also; they did, but not often. If after talking with the child, my degree of suspicion remained high, I would ask them for a urine specimen. A refusal to do so often provided the information needed to move forward, no secret testing required.

Some parents asked me about cutting their child's hair to test the child for drugs. I was against this on principle, but parents sometimes did not care for my advice. It addition to its being a "violation" of the child of sorts, this approach, I told them, provides information that reflects past use and, moreover, is unlikely to pick up light users and recent use.

In our phone calls, I mentioned the tragic death of one young man in my practice from a heroin overdose. One reason some physicians choose pediatrics is that death is an uncommon outcome. Over my years of practice, I had patients die of complications of congenital malformations (4), leukemia (1), SIDS (2), drowning (1), auto accident (1), sledding accident (1), suicide (3), homicide (1), and drug overdose (1). A parent never imagines losing a child, and whatever consolation I was able to provide I knew was small comfort at best. These were the worst days of my practice career.

A week or so after this heroin overdose, another adolescent male was in my office for a follow up of his admission to an in-patient treatment center for heroin abuse. I had not been involved in his admission and had been unaware of his substance-abuse problem. I asked him to help me understand how I could have known about his problem or my other patient's abuse of this very dangerous drug prior to getting the phone call about his death. He told me I could not know. They would have hidden it. I suppose that is true though I wish it were not.

LGBTQ youth (Lesbian, Gay, Bisexual, Transgender, Queer or Questioning)

The term LGBTQ came into use around 2005. How gender identification and sexual orientation issues will evolve is anybody's guess. Currently things are quite fluid. Whether our society ultimately looks upon these issues more through the lens of individual testimony, law, religion, art, or science remains to be seen.

Two terms might be helpful. Gender dysphoria—defined as discomfort, unhappiness, or distress due to one's gender or physical sex—relates to a mismatch between biological sex and gender identity (whether one sees oneself as a male or female). Sexual orientation relates to which gender (which sex) one is attracted to. Both of these issues are probably best viewed as more of a continuum than an either-or concept.

In an earlier chapter I spoke of a toddler who panicked when the garage door went up announcing the arrival of his father from work. Hurriedly, he tried to put away his "girl" toys (did this represent his gender identity or normal play?). In this chapter under sex and intimacy, I spoke of a woman who identified herself as heterosexual in orientation, but the only two "men" she'd had sex with were both biologically women (gay?). I have taken care of young men who saw themselves as women and young women who saw themselves as men. I had a 14-year-old male come in for his annual checkup and when he took off his clothes he was wearing his sister's underwear (fantasy play or gay male?). I have received phone calls from parents of gay youth who wish for therapy to change their child.

LGBTQ youth are normal, just different. Every child with a distinctive gender identity or choice in sexual orientation needs support, especially from parents. When discussing these issues with parents, I would always start with the wellbeing of the child in their own home. Can both parents accept their child for however the child identifies themselves by gender and for however they chose to express themselves in their intimate sexual relationships? When this does not occur, the outcome is often quite damaging.

I would then turn to the child or adolescent themselves. What information, if any, would they like to have from me? Some wished to explore hormonal and surgical options. Some were experiencing emotional distress and needed to talk to someone. Sometimes this information was shared confidentially by the patient and they simply wanted my help in telling their parents.

Not all pediatricians will be equally comfortable with these issues. Nor are all pediatricians competent to treat various issues that may arise. In these cases, expect to be referred to a specialist. If the issues are physical or there is an expressed desire to consider hormonal therapy, this referral might be to an endocrinologist who specializes in transgender youth. If the issues are psychological, the individual might be a psychiatrist or psychologist who specializes in these issues (transparentusa.org/resources/find-local-resources).

Science is likely to surprise us in this area. I suspect we will learn that biology is at play when individuals define themselves with different gender identities than their biological sex or find themselves attracted sexually to different sexes than we might traditionally predict. We all need to be open to learning more about these matters and be accepting as we move forward so that in the future children and adolescents will no longer have to traumatically "come out" and be seen as different. My overwhelming goal when working with LGBTQ youth was the same that it was when working with all adolescents—that they develop a high level of self-esteem and self-acceptance and have strong connections to family and the community in which they live.

Coping with stress—conversion reactions, school avoidance and somatic complaints, and eating disorders

Stress was often at the root of many "medical" problems that presented to my office during the adolescent years. Most kids handled it well with the occasional meltdown thrown in. Others struggled to manage it by developing maladaptive coping strategies including conversion reactions, school avoidance (with recurrent somatic complaints), and eating disorders.

Where is all this stress coming from? Almost everywhere, it turns out. Ambitious students are at risk when ambition becomes perfectionism. The perfectionist cannot tolerate failure and feels inadequate. However, one does not need to be the ambitious, perfectionist student to find school stressful. Stress from school is a more or less uniformly reported complaint from teens, and this can intensify with college acceptance hanging over their heads. Some athletes experience the same kind of perfectionist stress when pushed too hard by themselves, their parents, or their coaches. Many of them have been programmed to pursue a college scholarship since entering team sports and are often encouraged or even pressured to pick a single sport to "specialize" in at a young age. In addition to school and sport-related stress, being successful socially can be a 24/7 job. It used to be that a teenager could come home from school and get away from the pressures of social life. But social media never takes a day (or night) off and can be associated with bullying and FOMO (fear of missing out). Many adolescents pursue popularity instead of real friendship. The former is hard to achieve and can lead to anxiety and "drama" while the latter can be protective, from a stress creating point of view, and contribute to better overall mental health. I would often ask teens if they had a "best friend" and was pleased if they did pointing out to them that a few close relationships were usually more valuable than being popular. These close relationships allow for practicing intimacy skills needed throughout life like reading social cues, having empathy for others, learning how to communicate in difficult situations, and how to forgive and forget.

Some households are more stressful than others as children are exposed to marital issues including divorce, parents with mental-health and substance-abuse problems, financial strain, and at times a parent with a life-threatening physical illness. All of this is on top of the need to filter the constant barrage that all of us feel of national and world events involving terrorism, war, catastrophe, school shootings, and politics.

In my experience, the biggest stress affecting kids is meeting their perception of what we as parents expect them to achieve. We know they will and need to make mistakes. We know they will not be proficient at every task in front of them; after all, they still have a lot of growing up to do. Their grades will not be perfect and they will lose some ballgames along the way. But often, this is not what they perceive and feel. Inadvertently, parents can sometimes be sending a different message. My daughter at this age came home with a fabulous report card—straight A's, as usual. There was a comment from the teacher that perhaps she could share more of her ideas in the class. Being shy, this was not her nature. I praised her for her grades but also mentioned the teacher's observation about sharing her ideas. I think all she took away from my comments was my disappointment. Blew that one!

Many adolescents have little experience with failure and lack the resilience needed to succeed in the adult world. This fear of failure has become an epidemic result of a generation of children raised by well-meaning but anxious, helicopter parents, parents who at times, in order to avoid feeling the hurt of their child's disappointments, intervene to "prevent" the very failure that might result in the most powerful lessons their child could hope to learn.

As a pediatrician, many days seemed repetitive . . . check-ups, earaches, strep throat. But then someone would come in with symptoms that sounded pretty serious, and yet, just a little off. What do I mean by a little off? The symptoms were usually "neurological" with some of the following: muscle weakness or paralysis, sometimes abnormal movements or what sounded like seizures, loss of consciousness at times, or changes in vision or hearing. Yet extensive medical examinations and testing, when necessary, did not confirm a physical illness or what doctors call an organic cause. If your doctor is on their toes, they might start asking about stressful events and suspect that the stress or trauma has been "converted" to physical symptoms. The mind can play tricks on itself. A diagnosis of a conversion reaction can often be traced back to a psychological trigger.

To illustrate, here are the histories of two such patients in my practice:

- A 17-year-old presented to the emergency room with involuntary body movements (choreoathetosis), dizziness, and an unsteady gait. He had a past medical history of concussions from football and a sibling with a brain tumor. He complained of not being able to keep his legs from moving. A neurologist was consulted and admitted him to the ICU thinking these were seizures. However, brain wave testing (EEG) and brain scans (MRI) were normal. This is what occurs in conversion reactions. An unusual story with some dramatic physical signs, yet normal testing. The only question was where the stress was coming from; in this case it was from schoolwork.

- A 16-year-old girl presented to the emergency room for evaluation of a fainting spell (syncope). She had been playing lacrosse immediately prior to fainting. She was "dazed" for 30 minutes afterward and had to be carried to the car, as she was unable to walk. Mentally, she returned to normal but complained of being unable to use her arms or legs. Similar events had continued for almost a year by the time I saw her. Some days her fainting might occur six to seven times. Other days not at all. The fainting never happened while she was alone. Multiple neurologic studies were performed and all were normal. The only identifiable stress had been her desire to please her parents and, in her own words, "not cause them all the problems my older brother did."

Of the two patients, the 17-year-old required a minor degree of psychiatric or psychological care. He seemed to be relieved that his symptoms were, so to speak, all in his head. The young woman required a more prolonged course of treatment that called for ongoing counseling and medication.

School avoidance is a more typical presentation for many young people dealing with stress. It usually starts in the early teen years and is seen more frequently in boys than girls. Typically, children dealing with school avoidance issues have recurrent and vague physical (somatic) complaints. The symptoms are more common on Mondays and in the morning when it is time to go to school. And yet, at their office visits, these patients have a normal examination. One creative adolescent was faking fevers (factitious fevers) by rolling the thermometer in his hand when the mother left the room at home. Another, I came to think, wanted to stay at home to emotionally protect his mother as his stepfather was no longer in the home. A third came from a home with a strong family history of anxiety. His anxiety involved most all social activity, and his parents simply could not make him attend school.

He never admitted to being bullied, but I believed that was the source of his stress. This refusal to go to school went on for two years as the school made many accommodations, perhaps enabling him somewhat.

While school avoidance might seem to be a relatively minor issue, in fact it isn't, and should not be shrugged off by your pediatrician. Your physician needs to take a very careful history and perform a thorough examination if your child is exhibiting this behavior. If the results are normal, as parents, you should expect that the advice will be for your child to return to school immediately. Also, it is important for you to anticipate that Mondays and mornings will be the most common time to hear about physical complaints and, if you cannot get your child to school, take them to the doctor's office for an examination as soon as possible so that they might still be able to attend school that day.

If I could only ask a single question of each family at a checkup, it would be, how many days of school have you missed this year? It would tell me a lot about how the adolescent is functioning. It would also give me some insight into how the household is functioning. At this age, school is the adolescent's job. Studies show that kids with high rates of school absenteeism have less success in their working careers. When the problem becomes chronic, and it frequently does, a referral to a mental health specialist may be necessary to work on deeper issues in both the adolescent and the household.

Eating disorders are complex, and, in contrast to school avoidance, they are more common in girls than in boys. An eating disorder often takes a perfect storm to develop: a teen, struggling with stress and perfectionism, is trying to gain control of their life often in the context of being anxious and having issues of self-esteem. Treatment consists of individual, group, and family psychotherapy, nutritional counseling, and, at times, medication. It also occasionally requires hospitalization to re-feed patients; there are specialized residential settings to treat these patients as well. Most people do not realize that it takes, on average, seven years to overcome an eating disorder. During this long period, the primary job of the family and health-care team, in my opinion, is to keep them safe until they develop what Freud called the "ego strength" to leave this controlling behavior behind. An excellent book for family and friends of those with eating disorders is *Surviving an Eating Disorder*, by Michele Siegel, Judith Brisman, and Margot Weinshel.

As I have said, the hallmark of pediatric care is prevention. Caring for kids where the stresses of life are being expressed in the form of conversion reactions, school avoidance with multiple somatic complaints, and eating disorders can be very difficult. But if we accept that all children are facing stress in their lives, we can teach them to manage this stress and develop a strong sense of self. This age is a time to develop lifetime values with some depth (compassion for others, honesty, fairness, commitment to family and work) in such a way that the minor disappointments in life do not rule the day. As parents, we must appropriately model how to deal with stress and use teachable moments with our children to allow them to accept some failure and disappointment as part of life. Shame and feelings of inadequacy need to be replaced by self-esteem. Finally, we must recognize and become more aware of the messages we are sending to our children about our expectations and aspirations for them socially, in school, and in the extra-curricular activities they choose. The pressure they feel from their parents, often due to the teen's misreading of what parents say and do, cannot be underestimated.

Depression

The previous section about teens discussed stress and some of its more unusual manifestations such as conversion reactions, school avoidance, and eating disorders. When I first started in practice, I had no idea that ultimately my time as a pediatrician would be dominated by attending to mental health concerns and assisting families to manage psychosocial problems.

Depression is particularly important as the risk of suicide is real. As I mentioned above in a prior section, three young people did take their own lives during my practice career. Two of these adolescents were under psychiatric care for depression while one was not at the time of his death. Not often does a teenage patient call the office to ask for help with depression. Likewise, parents may not initiate the conversation because they are unaware of their adolescent's depression or embarrassed to bring up a mental health problem. For these reasons, it's imperative that pediatricians screen all kids in their offices for the signs that put some adolescents at risk. It's also important to recognize when there are factors at work in an adolescent's environment that can actually be protective of good mental health. Doctors should actively identify these strengths and build on them.

The HEEADSSS method of interviewing adolescents can be used in the office at a check-up. (contemporarypediatrics.modernmedicine.com/ contemporary-pediatrics/content/tags/adolescent-medicine/heeadsss-30-psychosocial-interview-adolesce?page=full). This assessment tool developed by Klein, Goldenring, and Adelman consists of open-ended questions about home, education and employment, activities, drugs, sexuality, suicidality, and safety which allows pediatricians to explore factors that would suggest a teenager is at risk—or has characteristics of resilience. Though we must attend to known risk factors, over the years I tried to spend more time trying to identify the protective factors present in an adolescent's life and praise these personal, family, and community strengths.

During my years in practice, I always found one individual assessment in the HEADSSS screen particularly critical: employment. Some kids "need" to work to contribute to the economic needs of their family. At times, work gives kids additional responsibility or fills what might be idle time (to get into trouble). But my experience was that often, at this age, work outside the home was a detriment. Sometimes it brought kids into contact with young adults who were not on the trail of success. Sometimes it gave them spending money that was used for the wrong reasons. Sometimes it took them away from their most important job—performing well in school. There are only so many hours in the day. I would rather see them devoted to areas that are known to be protective of good mental and social health—good school performance, involvement in sports and youth groups, or charity work in the community.

I mentioned that depression can present with a straightforward phone call from a parent or the patient themselves. But it is also now a part of routine pediatric practice to screen for depression. In my group practice we used the PHQ-9 questionnaire (phqscreeners.com/sites/g/files/ g10016261/f/201412/PHQ-9 English.pdf). Patients are asked to answer nine questions about how they have been feeling over the past two weeks. They grade each area 0, 1, 2, or 3 (not at all, several days, more than half the days, and nearly every day). The questions represent the core symptoms of depression:

- Little interest or pleasure in doing things
- Feeling down, depressed, or hopeless
- Trouble falling asleep, staying asleep, or sleeping too much
- Feeling tired or having little energy
- Poor appetite or overeating
- Feeling bad about yourself or that you have let yourself or your family down
- Trouble concentrating on things such as watching TV or reading the paper
- Speaking or moving more slowly such that other people notice it; or the opposite: being fidgety or restless and moving around a lot more than usual
- Thoughts that you would be better off dead or of hurting yourself in some way

A total score of 0-4 suggests no reason for concern; 5-9, mild depression; 10-14, moderate depression; 15-19, moderate-to-severe depression; and 20-27, severe depression. Those with moderate-to-severe and severe depression need a therapeutic plan. Those in the mild and moderate categories might require therapy as well, depending on the duration of symptoms and the degree of impairment these symptoms are causing.

When depression is suspected, it needs to be diagnosed definitively, and like any other disease, proper therapy should be initiated. This includes educating the family about depression, strongly insisting upon the patient's starting counseling with cognitive behavioral therapy, and considering medications (although their presumed benefit in the adolescent population is not without controversy). Patients need to be asked if they have plans to hurt themselves as this might indicate a medical emergency. In addition, family histories of suicide can place a patient at further risk and additional history needs to be obtained about possible physical or sexual abuse.

Occasionally, a given community may experience a rash of suicides that unnerves parents. At other times, a film, book, or TV program may almost seem to glamorize this tragedy (the TV series 13 Reasons Why could be considered an example) and may have this effect on parents and students alike. These are opportunities to be seized. Do not be afraid to openly discuss suicide with your child if they are suffering from depression. Remind them that, together, you can seek treatment for their issues. Remind them that suicide is final. If your religious faith is strong and suggests only God decides when you die, share those feeling as well.

A serious issue related to, but not to be confused with, suicide is cutting or self-mutilation. Those attempting and committing suicide are trying to end all feelings, whereas cutters are using self-inflicted pain to feel better. Though these may be depressed patients or have other serious mental-health diagnoses, they also may not be. Cutting behaviors are often "contagious," so to speak, and learned from friends. My experience with these young people suggests they either give the behaviors up quickly or start to act out impulsively in other ways as well. I would advise calling your pediatrician to discuss cutting behaviors, as they often will require some combination of behavioral and pharmacologic therapy. However, do not worry that the child is necessarily at risk for suicide.

Adolescent Safety

We have already touched on several adolescent safety issues when discussing substance use, dating violence, and depression. But a couple of additional safety issues deserve special attention.

The leading cause of death in adolescents is auto accidents. In fact, the CDC states that 16-19 year olds are three times more likely to die per hour driven than those 20 and older. What puts them at such high risk and can these risk factors be ameliorated? There are five main contributors: lack of universal seat belt use, ingestion of any alcohol, inexperience, distracted driving from electronic devices or additional passengers in the car, and night time driving. Some fixes might come from inventive technology to ensure seat belt use, not drinking and driving, and making cell phones inoperable while a car is moving. Until the last of these becomes a reality, we all need to turn off our cell phones when driving. Time, practice, and curfews can help with inexperience and night time driving. Some state laws do limit the number of passengers that young drivers can transport. Again, parental presence is required for these risks to be addressed consistently.

119

A second special issue in adolescent safety takes dating violence one step further to sexual violence. Women are more often victims than men though not exclusively so. Often the perpetrator is known to the victim. They might be a contemporary, but could also be a family member or family friend. If this occurs, do contact your pediatrician immediately to arrange for medical treatment and psychological support. The police should be notified as well.

As parents, we are very aware of how "sexualized" our culture has become. We must expect that adolescents will explore how they might choose to participate and act in this environment, yet remain safe. As I prefer to provide care for adolescents into their college years, it became necessary to provide some advice to minimize the risk of unwanted sex. Some suggestions seemed clear cut. There should be no sexual activity between two people who just met and are drinking. If there is real interest in dating, re-connect the next day when sober. And while out drinking, both males and females need to carefully watch their drinks to ensure that no one adds a date rape drug (rohypnol) without their knowledge. When going out with a group to a party, return home with the group as well. And finally, be clear in your communications with what you want. Colleges are starting to make consent a matter of "yes means yes" rather than "no means no". This might help. There can be no blaming the victim when sexual violence occurs but let's reduce the risk and follow the advice offered above.

A host of adolescent safety issues are well addressed by the Center for Disease Control. See their website: cdc.gov/parents/teens/safety.html.

Sleep

I recall the time a mother contacted me to say that her high school daughter, who was a good student and played on the field hockey team, was falling asleep in her classes. The mother said her daughter went to bed after midnight on school nights, staying up to do homework and talking to friends. She said her daughter had trouble falling asleep and went to bed with music on and her cell phone by her side. On the weekends, her daughter did not get out of bed until afternoon. The mother asked if this was this normal and what suggestions I might have for her.

I explained that adolescents require at least nine hours of sleep a night and that they usually do not feel tired at 9 or 10 o'clock, making it nearly impossible to get enough sleep if they have to get up at 6 or 7 in the morning to get to school. The body's internal clock (circadian rhythms) changes normally at this age and can negatively affect sleeping patterns, which, in turn, can have an impact on attentiveness and learning in school. While some schools have tried to address this problem with later start times, such an approach has not been widely adopted, which is a mystery to me.

Not only can this lack of sleep have measurable effects on working memory, attention span, and reaction time, it can have tragic results for someone driving late at night. Sleep deprivation has also been blamed for exacerbating feelings of depression and anxiety.

What steps can parents take to keep their child's body clock running "on time"?

1. They should not let them "sleep in" on the weekend, other than, perhaps, an extra hour or so. Sleeping in longer doesn't result in "catching up" and has been shown to extend weeknight sleepiness to even later hours.

2. They should tell their child to only use their bed to sleep. It is not a "location" for studying, listening to music, or staying connected with friends through social media. Just as with an infant or child, a good sleep routine is critical and could include reading quietly and staying off social media and video games for at least an hour before lights out. And once the child goes to bed, all devices should be silenced, and if necessary, turned over to you until the morning.

3. There should be no naps after school (and certainly not in class). Napping can interfere with their already disordered circadian rhythm.

4. If their child is taking stimulant medications for ADD/ADHD that have resulted in insomnia, discuss this problem with your pediatrician. It may be possible to alter the medications to reduce their duration of action or to add melatonin, a natural hormone produced by the brain which may help with insomnia.

We all need to make choices about what is important and it can be hard to "make" a teenager conform to sleep rules such as these. It usually works best when the child agrees to these changes by themselves.

Should adolescents attending college leave a pediatric practice?

Many pediatricians require adolescents to leave their practice at age 18. It is not a matter of right or wrong, but I preferred that patients remain in my practice until college was completed. This was even more important when they were attending a college away from home. Those attending school in their home town could often make the change to an internist or family-medicine physician more successfully, as their occasional need for medical care might allow for enough visits to create continuity and an opportunity to establish a good doctor-patient relationship.

For those attending school away from home, episodic care often occurs in the student health center, so there is no opportunity to develop a relationship with a new physician. Furthermore, they cannot take advantage of the quality doctor-patient relationship that they have cultivated with their pediatrician over the first 18 or so years of life. For these students and their parents, I was a phone call away for advice about medical care and the occasional need for help with a confidential psychosocial problem. I hope your pediatrician allows and encourages your adolescent to stay in the practice till well past the age of 18.

Pet peeves or what was most challenging during this period of development

The stakes are awfully high with adolescents. These young men and women need to make independent choices in order to grow up, yet they are still developing adult judgment skills. Many people assume that adolescents take more risks because they feel invulnerable. Not all research supports that view. Perhaps it is more about being inexperienced in making choices.

More and more often, it seems that parents allow the adolescent themselves, along with the more-permissive parents in their immediate community, to make up the rules. Unreasonable and often unlawfully late curfews, mixed-sex sleep-overs, serving alcohol in the home, lack of supervision of social media, trying to be your adolescent's best friend— these are examples of what concerned me during my working years. There are real safety issues here.

But controlling parents can be problematic as well. The goal for adolescents should be for them to make many of their own decisions responsibly and become self-reliant. When parents cannot manage their own anxiety over their adolescent's safety, they often choose to disregard and invade boundaries, thereby preventing their children from reaching the very goal of growing up.

What would a healthier situation look like? How can you manage these years more successfully? When setting limits, can the dynamic seem less like a "power play" by the parent and more like a discussion where each side has input— before, ultimately, the parent decides? The answers might look like this:

1. Show your adolescent love and respect but do set limits if their safety is at risk or they lack the emotional development to manage a particular situation or choice. Do not allow other parents or the "community" to decide where you will need to draw the line.

2. Set a good example. If you want your child to make good choices, you must model the right behaviors 24/7.

3. Avoid decisions that are mostly about control and work on dealing with your own anxieties. If the child's choice is not truly unsafe, and they are emotionally mature enough to understand the ramifications of that choice, perhaps you need to allow them to make it. If things do not go well, it may represent a good opportunity for learning and growth.

4. Surprise them from time to time. Check in on where they said they intended to be.

5. Get to know the adults in their life. This might include their coaches, teachers, best friend's parents, neighbors, and co-workers if they have a job.

6. Sometimes, especially as they mature, they will ask for your opinion before making a decision. Offer it without judgment and give them alternatives to consider.

7. Expect them to break some rules and make some mistakes. Decide together in advance what will be reasonable consequences. Perhaps extenuating circumstances are involved and your adolescent had to consider additional issues not previously discussed and made a fairly responsible choice that still broke some household rules. Those are the times when you might need to show some flexibility.

Chapter 7

CHILDREN WITH SPECIAL NEEDS

We have covered a lot of ground but children with special needs cut across all the age groups I have discussed. Some have intellectual and cognitive challenges. Some have chronic medical diseases such as diabetes, cystic fibrosis, seizure disorders, psychiatric disorders, asthma, inflammatory bowel disease, or birth defects (congenital malformations) of an organ system such as the heart, brain, skeleton, or skin. Some have cancer and face a shortened life expectancy. Others have cancer and will survive but experience complications from chemotherapy or radiation later in life. Fortunately, many more with cancer will achieve remission and lead a normal life thanks to advances in therapies learned from clinical trials in the past.

Let's start with a couple of stories from my practice, as I learned more from caring for these children than I could have possibly contributed.

1. A family became my patients with two healthy boys and a third with Dandy-Walker syndrome. This is a rare birth defect of the brain leading to hydrocephalus (fluid within the brain) and significant motor and intellectual delays. Some of these children have seizures as well. A fourth pregnancy resulted in another child affected by the same condition. These boys are now in their twenties. The care they have received from their parents has been extraordinary and their willingness to share their wisdom and the details of daily life with me has been enlightening.

2. A four-year-old boy presented to my office with weight loss, thirst, and frequent urination. A test revealed a diagnosis of diabetes. His 11-year-old brother broke down in tears when I informed his mother of the results of the test. He had diabetes himself and did not want his brother to have it.

3. An old friend asked me to be her family's pediatrician. Her second of three pregnancies resulted in a girl with Down syndrome. Five days after giving birth, the mother and her husband had to return to the hospital for treatment of a fluid leak from the mother's spinal anesthesia. Standing at the elevator with their daughter in their arms, the parents overheard two candy-stripers involved in a conversation with their backs to the family. One of the two girls seemed to be "in charge," giving instructions. When the two girls turned around, the girl in charge had the typical facial features of someone with Down syndrome. Neither parent spoke to the other until they were back in the car when they agreed that this was "serendipity and a scene in life just meant for us" and a "sign of hope."

4. Prior to routine newborn screening for nearly 35 medical conditions, including cystic fibrosis, a family came to see me for a second opinion about their four-month-old son who had diarrhea and was growing poorly. A sweat test confirmed my suspicion of cystic fibrosis. The boy was referred to experts at a local university teaching hospital where state-of-the-art therapy has allowed him to lead a normal life some 18 years later with but a single hospitalization.

These families and many others like them, not I, became the experts on their conditions as I spent a fair amount of time at each of their visits asking them questions to better understand some of these rare diseases and, more importantly, how they had changed their lives. The mother who saw the sign of hope in her child with Down syndrome gave me a book titled *Changed by a Child,* edited by Barbara Gill, a moving collection of essays in which families share their perspectives on parenting children with special needs.

Two sets of circumstances stood out most for me in Gill's book. The first was the notion that these parents wished to outlive their children. Who would care for them otherwise?

The second was how much contact these families would have with the medical system. Unfortunately, despite the assumption that the medical community is best positioned to be understanding and empathetic, there were times when individual encounters brought forth anything but understanding and empathy. This helped me stay focused on offering not just treatment, but compassion.

What advice did I give to parents that seemed most helpful?

- The greatest limitations placed on any child, with or without special needs, are the ones parents place upon them themselves. Do not underestimate what your child will be able to accomplish.

- Become an expert on your child's medical condition. The rarer the condition, the more important such expertise can be. How you choose to learn will vary from family to family. It may involve attending conferences in your home town or internationally. It may involve joining a parent support group or asking your pediatrician if a family with a similar condition in their practice would be willing to meet and discuss what the diagnosis has meant in their life and the life of their child and their family. The internet is a resource as well, but as stated earlier, not all information or websites are equal in their trustworthiness. This reservation should be balanced against often very helpful advice and tips from other families with a child who has a similar condition. Ask your pediatrician for recommended resources and parent groups accessible on the web.

- Be an advocate for your child when working with both the medical and school community.

- Be willing to teach, inform, and train others in your community about children with special needs. Your story is likely a powerful one and will help all of us be better prepared to face our own family's medical challenges.

- Do not expect everyone in your usual circle of support to "get it" when it comes to supporting you and your child. Sometimes the people you expect most of, family and close friends, will disappoint you. Strangely, this is often offset by unexpected support and compassion from others you would not think to count on. Be open to their help and their desire to be close to you and your child.

- Make sure your pediatrician stays involved. Your child may need to have much of their medical care provided by specialists, but a pediatrician can monitor things and be a respected advocate for your child making certain that all matters, large and small, are attended to.

And what about the other kids in the family without special needs? My impression, which is supported by these parents, was there were pros and cons. The pros where compassionate, kind, understanding, and accepting young people who did not hesitate to help others in the community and even pitch in to give their parents a break to care for a sibling when needed. In addition, their experience with more serious medical conditions allowed them to develop some medical competence that would likely prove valuable when raising their own children. But cons exist too. These siblings have their own issues, and though not necessarily real, at times they might feel that their needs came second or that simple pleasures like family vacations or family activities might not occur as planned. Some kids even act out inappropriately to get more attention. On balance, most parents would tell me that the pros outweighed the cons in any event and the siblings, when asked, confirmed that opinion.

Chapter 8

FINAL THOUGHTS

One of my favorite office visits were the prenatal interviews. I would schedule these at the end of the day so that my time with the parents-to-be was unlimited. During these interviews, I would obtain some family history, answer questions about my practice, create reasonable expectations for the new parents, and make sure doctor and patients were a good fit for each other.

At the end of one interview, a father asked me a simple question that no one had ever asked: If I could give him and his wife one piece of advice, what would it be? My answer was simple: Do your best and accept that.

People study and train to do their jobs and feel competent that they can do them well. But faced with the most important job of our life, parenting, we commence without formal education or training. This is just one hurdle.

Another hurdle is that we do not want to do our job well, we want to do it *perfectly*. This is just not possible. Your parents did not. Their parents did not. Your neighbors will not. I did not. Take a deep breath and free yourself of that thought. Is it gone? I hope so. If it is, you will be happier, and your children will be better off, for it.

Over the years, Christmas Eve was a special time for my wife and me. After getting the kids to bed, we would pull out the toys we had purchased and start laughing at the three most dreaded words in the English language—*Some Assembly Required*. As I wrote this "little book" about savvy parenting advice, those words took on a different meaning as I reminded myself what a unique opportunity it is to raise a child!

Let's not forgot some of the key points in our conversation:

1. Develop parental presence. The greatest gift to your child is your time and your attention.
2. Work with your pediatrician as a partner and share all information that might be helpful.
3. Be aware of your own anxieties and manage them.
4. Be intentional about demonstrating and teaching your own values.
5. Make an effort to understand how you were raised and identify and address unresolved issues that might affect your parenting decisions. Then get on the same page with your partner if you can.
6. Set limits consistently but with love and respect. Allow your children, as they become older, to become increasingly self-reliant and responsible for their decision making.
7. Monitor the acquisition of developmental assets and consider how best to address significant gaps.
8. Support your child but let them face their adversities and develop the inner strength and character they will need to be successful, resilient adults and a vital part of their communities. You must anticipate and accept some mistakes as they are often the best opportunity for personal growth.

Now, sit back and enjoy each and every day. You have the best seat in town.

List of referenced books

1. *Parenting From the Inside Out,* by Daniel Siegel and Mary Hartzell
2. *Solve Your Child's Sleep Problems,* by Richard Ferber
3. *The Happiest Baby on the Block,* by Harvey Karp
4. *Caring for Your Baby and Young Child,* by the American Academy of Pediatrics
5. *Touchpoints,* by T. Berry Brazelton
6. *Identity and the Life Cycle,* by Erik Erikson
7. *Your Child's Health,* by Barton Schmitt
8. *The Difficult Child,* by Stanley Turecki
9. *Driven to Distraction,* by Edward Hallowell
10. *Motivational Interviewing,* by Stephen Rollnick
11. *How To Talk So Kids Will Listen & Listen So Kids Will Talk,* by Adele Faber and Elaine Mazlish
12. *Surviving an Eating Disorder,* by Michele Siegel, Judith Brisman, and Margot Weinshel
13. *Changed by a Child,* edited by Barbara Gill

List of referenced websites

1. parentsasteachers.org
2. pediatrics.aappublications.org/content/early/2016/10/20/peds.2016-2938
3. immunize.org
4. chop.edu
5. ncbi.nlm.nih.gov/pubmed/24814559)
6. aap.org
7. babycenter.com
8. myfoodplate.gov
9. (media.chop.edu/data/files/pdfs/vaccine-education-center-autism.pdf
10. autismspeaks.org/what-autism/treatment/applied-behavior-analysis-aba)
11. cdc.gov/getsmart/community/for-hcp/outpatient-hcp/pediatric-treatment-rec.html
12. nichq.org/childrens-health/adhd/resources/vanderbilt-assessment-scales)
13. brightfutures.org/mentalhealth/pdf/professionals/ped_sympton_chklst.pdf).
14. cdc.gov/ncbddd/adhd/diagnosis)
15. cdc.gov/ncbddd/adhd/guidelines))
16. chadd.org
17. splitfilm.org
18. search-institute.org/what-we-study/developmental-assets://search-institute.org/what-we-study/developmental-assets)

19. wikipedia.org/wiki/Tannerscale)
20. childrenshospital.org/ceasar/crafft/screening-questionnaire
21. transparentusa.org/resources/find-local-resources)
22. contemporarypediatrics.modernmedicine.com/contemporary-pediatrics/content/tags/adolescent-medicine/heeadsss-30-psychosocial-interview-adolesce?page=full
23. phqscreeners.com/sites/g/files/g10016261/f/201412/PHQ-9 English.pdf)
24. cdc.gov/parents/teens/safety.html.